# SARAH HILL

# Where Did You Learn To Behave Like That?

*A Coaching Guide for Working with Leaders*

Copyright: Dialogix 2017

ISBN: 978-1-9998217-0-8

Published with CreateSpace Independent Publishing Platform.

Cover design: Rachel Horton-Smyth with Alex Thomas

Cover images: © iStockPhoto.com

For the determined, resolute, beautiful child in the adult,
whose fight to write a new narrative in life informs
every page of this book.

# Contents

# Introduction

Whether we can easily locate it or not, every one of us has a unique story of how we experienced love as children, which we bring with us into adulthood. That story powerfully influences our behaviour, affecting those around us in countless untold ways. Knowing one's own childhood story[1] and being truly in command of it goes to the very core of the challenge to make real and durable change happen in the social systems we all live and work in.

No-one's experience and memory of love as a child is perfect, and the story of those imperfections[2], whether large or seemingly trivial, impact our adult lives. *Where Did You Learn To Behave Like That?* provides a practical guide for coaches to work safely and effectively with these childhood stories. The goal in childhood story work is to equip us with the insight and skills necessary to achieve a real command of our own behaviour, especially under pressure. Going to work on the childhood stories of the past helps us to stop judging and blaming others – instead turning our attention to our own role and contribution to what is happening. This allows us to start on the road to becoming healthy, positive and truly developmental individuals, seeking to be more aware and skilful in all our social interactions.

We have probably all seen the wide-ranging and harmful impact of leaders[3] who have not had the opportunity to work on their childhood story, or who are unaware of its very existence and importance. The dysfunction can range from verbally lashing out at the people who are working to support them, to steamrolling or abandoning just when they are needed the most. We have probably all had manifestations of such behaviour in ourselves too, sometimes without noticing it fully. In these moments, it can be literally that the childhood story has entered the room, taken over and is doing harm – often with the individual completely oblivious to the source of their behaviour.

---

1 The term 'Story' using a capital 'S' is an abbreviation of 'childhood story' throughout.
2 As you will read later in the book, Stories of imperfect love can range from the seemingly trifling disappointments to the most horrific betrayal or abuse.
3 The working definition of 'leader' in this context is anyone who leads from where they are which means taking a lead from within any role. It is not a reference to hierarchical leadership.

## Bridging a gap and laying down a challenge

Many coaches and consultants describe how they feel unprepared to work with behaviour emanating from a leader's childhood story, or they do so purely instinctively. They may also not see any good reason for doing childhood story work. Unless therapeutically trained, they may not have suitable models for doing work of this kind, or there may be a gap in their Practice Model[4] that results in a feeling of being ill-equipped to do it. This book [and the training that accompanies it[5]] is intended to bridge that gap. This is achieved by taking the reader deep into the inner processes of working with the impact of childhood stories in an appropriate and skilful way.

The book provides a model for embarking on childhood story work with a leader, including the work that coaches and practitioners should do on their own Stories, before engaging deeply in childhood story work with clients. Within this is a central and fundamental challenge to coaches and consultants: that to work with leaders on their childhood stories as a 'Story-guide' [coach], practitioners must not just absorb the concepts and acquire the skills of childhood story work, but must also first be ready, willing and prepared to roll up their sleeves and go to work on their own childhood stories. This is crucial, because only through their own childhood story work can they achieve the level of [Self]-command that is so critical to being a truly effective facilitator of change in others.

Working on your own childhood story as a Story-guide can be particularly rewarding once you reach the stage of realising that you are out there doing good work in the world with your own childhood experiences playing a part, but without them hijacking the situation. You find yourself having an unprecedented level of awareness and command over those echoes from the past. This is hugely enabling for you, and your clients, because knowing your own childhood story deepens your capacity to understand the shadows in other people. One of the most poignant beauties of doing Story-work is gaining a profound understanding of what humans endure in the hands of other humans, while simultaneously having the requisite process-skills to remedy your clients' suffering, and help them transcend past damages.

---

4 A 'Practice Model' is defined by Kantor [2012] as a template of what the practitioner actually does in the room to make change happen.
5 Visit www.dialogix.co.uk/childhoodstory/for information about training.

## Introducing a model for working with childhood stories

Everyone has a childhood story of imperfect love. For example, the child was beaten, there was poverty or ill health in the family or education was prioritised over everything else in the family system. The facts of that childhood story do not change; they are immutable. However, there is also an existing [old] internal narrative that develops out of the immutable childhood story sub-consciously through to adulthood. This old internal narrative can cause devastation to the adult 'Self' and to others around us especially when we are in pressurised situations. An example of such an outdated internal narrative would be people taking responsibility for their beatings, their rejection or their failure to succeed, because [according to their outdated internal narrative] they did not then and do not today deserve any better.

Changing such negative power of the childhood story involves the adult changing the internal narrative about that Story. They obviously cannot change the Story itself, but they can change what the Story means for them. For example, they can realise that they were not worthless and therefore responsible for what happened, instead they were lovable, and should have been loved rather than being ignored, rejected or harmed.

In childhood story work, the Story-guide joins the 'Story-sharer' [client] in exploring the Story and the old internal narrative, creating increasing freedom from its power over the adult. The Story-guide asks the Story-sharer to pay attention to the behaviours they exhibit in their leadership so that they explicitly expand their knowledge and command of their potentially damaging behavioural inclinations. Together, they co-author a new internal narrative transforming the impact of the dark parts, so that they are still there, but no longer do harm. Note that this is very different from ignoring or suppressing them. Transcending the harm is what needs to happen. As a result of doing this, the person takes command of their internal narrative. By bringing the Story into the open, explicitly reflecting on its meaning with empathy and compassion, the childhood story no longer has the power to trigger involuntary patterns which derail and sabotage them in their adult lives.

By consciously changing the internal narrative, the Story-sharer robs the childhood story of its potentially negative power, and thereby finds a new kind of confidence, peace and ease in dealing with situations that previously evoked high stakes reactions and harmful behaviours in them. So first the Story-guide needs to set to work on helping the Story-sharer to find peace with the childhood story [especially peace with the fact that it did happen, and that nobody can make it 'un-happen']. They need to redeem the child, and this involves a degree of letting go of the old internal narrative so that it begins to become possible to write a new one.

The full model for working with childhood story is described in the chapters of the book that follow but inherent within it is a looping backwards and forwards. This looping back and repetitiveness is there – because that's what the essence of childhood story work involves. The real issue is deeper than the back-looping nature of childhood story work. It is the nature of the childhood story effects themselves – the very basic operating modes of the childhood stories in our mind that seem to be one big 'endless loop'. As a result, this keeps us stuck in place while we are desperately trying to move forward – and have often convinced ourselves that indeed we have 'moved on' – only to recognise later, that we are back to square one, back in the same mess all over again, when we thought we had left it behind.

When it comes to the looping nature of childhood story work, the film 'Groundhog Day' with Bill Murray reliving the same day over and over provides us with the perfect metaphor. This is because the film shows that progress is possible – albeit not easy – with every loop. It is hard to explain why it makes sense to go through almost the same thing over and over – because we so love dramatic breakthroughs – and are much less attuned to a continuous chipping away at things as beautifully described in the film. Even though the looping nature of childhood story work can be difficult to stick with, the fact that it is unfolding and full of potential are big motivators. In contrast, the nature of childhood story without childhood story work is much more like a 'closed loop' which has an incredible power to keep you locked in or to suck you back in. This is what childhood story does to us if we don't have the tools to work on it.

### Structure and foundations

The book has four main parts. In part one, you will read about the concepts that inform and underpin the terrain of childhood story. David Kantor's [1999, 2003, 2012] theory of Structural Dynamics and its application through a Practice Model developed over decades of coaching and intervention in this field provides the major conceptual foundation. Structural Dynamics is about how we communicate with one another and our behavioural preferences that drive the way we do this. It is a theory of face-to-face communication in low and high stakes. It provides the lens through which the Story-sharer can explain and understand their visible behaviour and what drives it, which is why it is a crucial foundation for this work.

The focus of childhood story work for coaches and consultants is on enabling the highest levels of what Kantor [2012] calls behavioural and communicative competence in themselves and the leaders they are working with – no matter how high the stakes might be. High stakes, in this context, means any situation, which causes anxiety or discomfort so intense that it invokes an almost involuntary behavioural response. In low stakes, we can be thoughtful, diverse and expansive in our behavioural choices. However, this changes as the stakes begin to rise, and the involuntary nature of our response can result in us wreaking havoc around us. The volatility of such spontaneous behaviours begins to explain the understandable struggles we often experience with how to respond when someone withdraws and abandons, threatens their closest friends or colleagues, or blames everyone else for what is failing.

Part two takes the reader into the process and practice issues of 'daring to ask' about childhood story. It explores, in practical terms, what it takes to enable someone to 'dare to look' at their childhood story and the impact it is having on their life. It offers guidance for coaches and consultants on what to do when someone appears to 'break down' or when the Story-sharer hits barriers in their childhood story work; not knowing how to explore them, not knowing if they even want to explore them.

The looping nature of childhood story work begins to show itself in part two when the complexities, twists and turns involved in going down this path become clearer. There is great merit and benefit in coming to know and understand the childhood story and its impact. Having done this, the Story-sharer may decide to pause or stop the work. However, should they decide to continue, the next phase of the work requires them to surface and become familiar with the internal narrative they developed in relation to the childhood story and this requires them to go even deeper in their exploration. Deep knowing of this old internal narrative can be extremely challenging, but is a critically important part of the process of being able to identify how that old internal narrative has served them well and how it has not.

Part three attends to what it takes to change the power of the childhood story and gain command of its accompanying old internal narrative through the writing of a new internal narrative. This involves skilful work on the part of the Story-guide, to help the Story-sharer lay down new pathways through dedicated work on the Self. In this section, you will again encounter the looping nature of childhood story work as intricate paradoxes and pitfalls appear. The Story-sharer inevitably encounters new aspects of the childhood story and its old narrative throughout the work. It is as though the childhood story and the old internal narrative come calling again and again. However, by this stage, the Story-sharer has become more and more equipped to deal with their appearance when they arrive and is able to integrate the learning that accompanies the experience to good effect.

In part four, the emphasis turns towards the deep and profoundly personal relationship between the Story-guide and the Story-sharer, including an exploration of the rewards, perturbances and intricacies that come with and through this unique and crucial relationship. The place and purpose of love in the relationship is discussed and questions are explored about reciprocity. This is also where the challenge to Story-guides to 'walk your talk', in other words, to do work on the Self too, is explained and explored in more depth and detail.

More generally, as you progress through the book you will notice a repeated looping backwards and forwards, as it takes you through similar, but not identical issues over and over again. This looping is actually reflecting the reality of Story-work itself. It is akin to walking a twisty but ultimately spiralling path up a hill, with many junctions, dead ends, clearings and even tunnels along the way. With each circuit, the view gets better, but it may be obscured along the way until eventually the view is unimpeded.

You may also notice the limits of language to convey the emotional, holistic experience that Story-work undoubtedly is. Story-work is complex, changeful and ambitious while a book – by its very nature is limited to language which is linear and precise. A book – even if it deals with Story-work in all its dimensions – cannot achieve the same kind of emotionally-holistic experience as, for example, a touch on the shoulder could. As you read the book, know that whilst what lies beneath the surface of the words may remain amorphous and indistinct at times, that 'touch on the shoulder' nevertheless is and should be fully present once you enter practical Story-work.

## Bringing Story-work to the fore

No book about childhood story would be complete without personal accounts of just what it takes to engage in Story-work. These feature throughout the book and I am deeply grateful to the leaders and coaches who have shared their experience so generously and without hesitation. Their generosity has allowed me to illuminate the practical process of Story-work in such rich detail and colour. Sometimes their quotes stand alone. At other times, they are used to explore the practical applicability of a particular idea or practice point.

In similar ways, my own Story also appears throughout the book and is an account of the Story-work I did with Story-guides who worked alongside me over several years. The Story-guide in my narrative represents elements from each of them as well as myself as a coach and interventionist. For the purposes of the book, I have called my Story-guide Michael. I felt a real dilemma about whether to identify myself the way I have done by incorporating my personal experience. However, what helped me decide was the realisation that, in doing so, I would be following my own advice. I made the choice to enact what I am espousing about the importance of knowing and being able to talk about your childhood story openly, without shame blocking and silencing you. This sounds simple and in a way it is, but it is also far from easy.

## A cautionary note

As you read the book, you may find yourself suddenly and perhaps unexpectedly caught in the grip of your own childhood story. This can be the result of connecting with the Stories of others shared here. Something you experienced as a child might be re-stimulated, or an aspect of your childhood story that you have perhaps avoided, discarded or forgotten, may suddenly surface. You may be confronted by strong feelings for the children within the stories you read – some of them are truly heart-breaking. Try to notice and catch yourself in the event of any of these things arising for you. Then reach out and talk with someone close to you who can help you to process what you are observing.

You may also find yourself questioning whether you actually have a childhood story, or you may compare your own childhood story to others' – perhaps judging it in some way, perhaps thinking it wasn't so bad, and you shouldn't make a fuss about it, especially with others having endured so much worse. If this happens for you, stop right there! More than anything else, I want to stress that absolutely everyone has a childhood story, and there is no single one that is better or worse than another, no single childhood experience of imperfect love that is more or less meaningful than another, no single childhood story that has more or less impact than another. The childhood story is unique to every individual and is intimately and inextricably bound up to our identity. This means that every childhood story is important and every childhood story has the potential to impact in untold ways and in the most inopportune of moments.

# PART ONE

*Examine The Ground*

# Chapter 1

## Feel The Impact

### A childhood story enters the room

*"A Story is ripest when events in the present raise resonant themes from the past, which rise to just below consciousness. From there, on provocation, they make their way into the room."*

**David Kantor**

**Invisible, yet present in more ways than one**

We know when a childhood story has entered the room because we all feel its impact. It is invisible, yet it is also vividly present, potentially doing harm to others and to ourselves. It frequently takes us by surprise at the most awkward of times. All it takes is for the stakes to go up just a little bit to trigger the childhood story into appearance. Before we know it, we are behaving in ways that confound and confuse even us, let alone the people who are on the receiving end of our subconscious behavioural patterns. In the aftermath of such events, as we reflect on what we said and did, the embarrassment or shame that is evoked by our behaviour can be hard to reconcile with our self-image. It can take days, weeks or even months to recover from such episodes.

We all have a childhood story of imperfect love, so it is unsurprising that there is a huge range in how imperfect love in childhood is experienced, from the smallest moments of disappointment or failure to the gravest abuse. Sometimes it can be hard to locate the presence or impact of the childhood story, but as Bridget describes, we know it when it's about to unleash turmoil:

> *I know when my childhood story is in the room, because I get a feeling. I know it because it's like no other. And I know if I have that feeling, I need to start looking for,*

'What's the childhood story here?' It's a feeling of being a little out of control. It's hard to describe because it's different than just being upset. There are plenty of things that make me upset where I'm not in the childhood story, but there's a particular feeling I get when I'm in it where I'm more emotional than the situation might need and I feel a little more out of control than the situation might suggest is necessary. I feel like I can't get myself understood. It's a funny fog that comes down around all that happens.

**Bridget, Coach**

In the account that follows we can hear just how much turmoil can be experienced when multiple childhood stories enter a room. However, one of the marked differences in this situation is that, unlike Bridget, neither the CEO, members of his team, nor the Consultant who was working with them, were aware of the presence or impact of their childhood stories in what they were experiencing:

Angus, CEO, concerned that the relationships across his Executive Team were becoming increasingly strained, asked for help from a team coach. He had noticed people becoming short-tempered and losing focus since a Board announcement to conduct a review into the ongoing effectiveness of a merger that had taken place two years earlier. The stakes were extremely high for him and the team as their performance was on the line.

A restructuring was going to reduce the team by 30% and Angus himself was facing the possibility of being axed. He described the team as historically having been strong and steady with a pretty stable membership, but talked about recent events having created a high degree of uncertainty and unpredictability that the team was struggling with.

Another external consultant had been brought in to provide support to the team about 18 months before. During this work, the relationships between team members and between the consultant and the team had broken down to such an extent that the intervention had had to be discontinued.

Angus's behaviour and another member of the team, Maggie, were both being scapegoated by colleagues who appeared to be blaming them for what was happening. During a visit to observe the team in action these behaviours played out and it was easy to see the dynamics in relation to Maggie. The stakes were so high for her that she started issuing threats to the consultant about what she would do if anyone tried to draw her into a conversation when the team was together. She was scared and uncomfortable with her colleagues and yet presented herself to them as confident, composed and slightly aloof.

Meanwhile, she was disclosing that there was real opposition to the process, the consultant and the methodology from other people in the team, and yet this was not being openly discussed. Maggie also talked about how previous consultants had seemed unable to deal with the dynamics in the team and that just as it had looked like they were getting close to something important, the team would see them off. There was a tale in the system that the dead bodies of the previous consultants who had tried and failed to work with them could be found in a locked room on the 17th floor of the headquarters building.

During one team session, Angus tried to draw his colleagues out from their reserve and spoke openly about what he was noticing. They stared blankly back at him, seemingly refusing to speak. In frustration, he raised his voice and began shouting at them, expressing in no uncertain terms his belief that they were the biggest single risk to the company and to his future career and that they needed to shape up or they would find themselves being shipped out. Then the finger pointing started, and members of the team turned on Maggie who in that moment became the sacrificial lamb for the group. Meanwhile, she sat stony-faced, staring into the distance. It seemed like she was completely inured to what was happening in the room. As the stakes escalated, another member of the team fled the room in tears with

*a colleague in hot pursuit seeking to comfort and rescue
her. As if the scene could not get any worse, two other
members of the team turned on the consultant and
laid into him, accusing him of all manner of things. In
that moment, just when he needed to hold the space,
step forward and work with what was happening in the
room, the consultant froze. It was as though his feet were
rooted to the spot, and for what seemed like an eternity it
seemed as though he had absolutely no idea which
way to turn or what to do.*

**Sarah, Author**

There is a lot going on in this scenario, including an out-of-control escalation of behaviours in crisis that became increasingly visible over time, but were acutely felt by everyone right from the start. What was also present, yet invisible, were the individual childhood stories of every one of the team members and the consultant working with them. These childhood stories were lurking behind the largely involuntary behavioural patterns playing out in the room; hidden Stories that were being triggered by the high stakes environment they all found themselves in. These Stories would do harm in all manner of overt and covert ways, so long as they remained activated, yet undiscovered.

## Sharing your Story: Singing defiance and freedom

Whilst knowing your Story and all the high stakes triggers that can result in it entering the room is core to Story-work, equally essential, is being able to share your childhood story with others. Challenging though it can be, the experience is like singing a voice of defiance and freedom. Each of the leaders and coaches who have shared their Stories and the experience of doing Story-work for this book were bold and courageous in the way they set to work on doing what was needed to really know themselves broadly and deeply. To achieve this was no small feat! So why do it at all? It started with an acute awareness of the potential harm they might easily do – inadvertently, yet no less devastatingly – when they caught sight of how the impact of their childhood story could at times lead to a proverbial mess in their interactions with others.

A commitment to minimise the potential harm from the impact of the Story to Self and others is such a powerful motivator to embark on the arduous but ultimately rewarding journey of Story-work. We hear in more detail what led Andrew, Ann, Donald and Samantha to engage in Story-work in their accounts below:

*I've got copious examples where something that's somewhat meaningless to somebody else, has actually been having a profound impact on myself and drawing me out of being in service of that system or that individual, and instead being so consumed in my own head, back in what is I now know to be childhood story. After having done work on Self and starting to understand some of my own childhood stories and work with those, I realised that it's not about stopping the Stories; it's about recognising them and being in control of them and then not letting them run too far. That makes it much easier to work with them. There's no switch, it's not about 'on or off', it's about awareness, ability to capture triggers, have mechanisms for extinguishing our own fires, and remaining able to do that relatively quickly to remain in service of either the individual you are with or the system you are working in.*

**Andrew, Leader**

*Over a long period of time I had various key points where I really wobbled. I would get very stuck. I would get very hurt in peoples' responses or I would be seeking approval a lot. It's taken years really, I'm about to turn 50. Every few months I'm leading a new group of people trying to work creatively and collaboratively, it's high stakes because it's original work. We have no idea whether the outcome will be good and it is millions of pounds of investment. It has to be successful, but not everything is   so there's a lot of pressure in the room. Working proactively with your childhood story in high stakes is a lovely process of learning about yourself. I was overly sensitive, overly responsive and overly reactive. I used to cope with that in different ways, but now I find myself much more able to just observe my own reactions. I was sitting in a meeting room the other day and I started to think, 'Ooh you've been talking too much. That's interesting. You're now going to edit yourself. What's the point of that, have you actually been talking too much or is this your younger Self remembering those things?'*

**Ann, Director**

*There will be themes in terms of how you have been parented, or the experiences you've had in your family that will frame significantly aspects of how you are as a leader. For everyone, there will be behavioural traits to work on. It comes down to being more aware in every situation of how you show up as a leader, and thinking about how you could be brave enough to behave slightly differently, or engage in a conversation slightly differently – often by describing how you think or how you feel – that leverages a different type of conversation with somebody else and ensures you do not inadvertently cause harm.*

**Donald, Chief Officer**

*I think that being in service of others is such an important part of a leadership model and, as part of that, being conversant with your own childhood story to be able to harness and work effectively with things that are coming up, in order to still be offering an effective leadership response or, enabling others, is so critical. And when you put it like that, why wouldn't you work on your Story, why wouldn't you want to be able to explore that more deeply?*

**Samantha, Leader**

Seeking to minimise potential harm was part of my own reasoning too. The process, which I embarked on to liberate my voice and heal the damage done by leftover hooks and habits of my childhood story was both tender and tough. The voice you will hear reflects my perspective on my childhood story, my lived reality, and my 'truth'. Yet of course, there will always be multiple realities and myriad perceptions of events. There will be different 'truths', sometimes many of them, with every one being valid from the specific standpoint of the Story-sharer or other characters, who feature in the childhood story. If either of my parents or my brother or sister were telling the 'same' story, there would, of course, be variations and differences in their accounts with each being no more or less 'true' than the other. What follows, however, begins my account of my childhood story and its impact on my personal and professional life as a leader, interventionist and coach, the trials and tribulations, the twists and turns of the Story-work – all that it took and all that it gave:

*I grew up in a family with a mum and a dad, a brother and a sister. I was the youngest child. My family was under constant pressure, because of poverty and my mother's physical ill health and depression that plagued us all in appalling ways. Along with my brother and sister, I was robbed of my childhood. We had to grow up fast to survive.*

*My Story is one of being abandoned, of not being protected, of not being looked after and of not being loved. Both of my parents physically beat me. I believed I had failed, because I let them do so. I believed I was responsible for the beatings. I fought back to them with my words sometimes. I got beaten more as a result. The feeling I had was of being worthless, soiled, something not wholesome, not good and not complete. I had no voice. I was completely isolated and silenced. I would walk into school with black eyes and lie about how I had got them.*

*I was caring for my mother from the age of seven. I couldn't say, 'take care of me' to her, because I was the carer for her. My father didn't protect me from her beatings. He joined in with them. The physical and emotional abuse I suffered at his hands was frequently borne out of his own frustration, anger and silent rage at her as well as himself for his failure to stand up to her. It got misdirected towards me.*

*I wanted to be a Human Rights Lawyer from a very early age. My mother would say, 'Well you will never become that, because you have to leave school as soon as you can and get a job to earn money and bring it into this house to continue living here.' I had my first job at the age of 12 as a waitress in a horrid, seedy little seaside cafe that the fishermen used to come to when they came off the boats in the early morning.*

*At around the age of 14, I fell prey to exploitation outside my family which resulted in me being brutally attacked and assaulted by two men. I was so traumatised and yet so isolated within my family, that I never told anyone what happened to me. Yet again, I did everything I could to hide the bruises.*

*There were aspects of my childhood story that were horrific and as an adult I needed to learn how to frame those experiences in a way to benefit my psychology, my capacity and myself. I set to work on learning to love myself. To do this, I needed to re-frame disaster. I needed to reframe myself from a damaged person to someone who is not. I needed to take the damage and do something good and whole and true with it that was in service of others and myself. Writing this book is one part of that.*

*As a child, I had killed a part of me in order to endure. Fully accepting as a grown-up that this was exactly what the child had had to do was critical to healing the harm of the Story and celebrating wholeheartedly the adult woman who is loved today. Before I began to work on my childhood story I, who knew how to love others, did not love the child within. In fact, I loathed and detested her. I had to learn to love her, to adore her, to exercise real love for her!*

*A core anchor of negativity about the Self, had been laid down. That's what my history did. That's what my parents did. The negativity was the basis of who I believed I was, the basis for what I did in the world and how I did it. How I loved came from that negative core, and yet what I came to discover was that the hundreds of things the child supposedly did wrong actually saved her life. The psychological and emotional knot I was dealing with was that I would not let up on the child in me, not even then, deep into adulthood. My own defence system that I had so wonderfully developed in childhood kept out danger, but it also kept out love. There was a void of love. Love became the enemy for the child, because she was confused about it, and the adult woman was too. Love was the thing she most desired and yet at the same time she saw it as her biggest enemy. If she let it into her life, she would be shockingly disappointed – again – getting the same kick she knew so well, the pain of which was seared into her memory until now. In summary: Keep the enemy out. Don't let love in! This became the centrepiece of my struggle against myself, as I finally began the hard work of dispelling this old internal narrative.*

*For as long as I can remember I have used my heart and mind to try to make up for my childhood experiences and I have worked so very hard to do that. This was much in evidence even in the early days of working on my Story. Episode after episode in my slowly unearthed internal narrative contained my unconscious challenge to the world:*

- *Can I speak back?*

- *Will people listen?*

- *Will I be heard?*

- *I need to be heard!*

*The connections between my childhood experience and all that I was doing professionally and personally became so clear. I was constantly setting out to overcome my childhood dilemmas, but until I went to work on the childhood stories themselves, I also kept running into all too familiar roadblocks that confused and frustrated me.*

**Sarah, Author**

The experience of those roadblocks – or rather the occurrences of my Story being triggered and all too frequently entering the room unwanted, unhelpful and often at the worst possible of moments – is where my

Story-work began in earnest. All that follows in the remaining chapters grew out of that experience and stems from the deep belief that it is necessary to have more people in this world who take their experience of imperfect love from childhood, drag it consciously into the open in adulthood and engage in the struggle to change the impact of that old Story, once they have managed to identify it. To do so, they will need the support of highly skilled practitioners who accompany them on their journey of discovery but this is how we truly can bring about different outcomes, healthier outcomes, better outcomes. Genuine freedom exists by going to work on the Stories of the past.

# Chapter 2

## Know The Context

### The archetypal childhood stories and other concepts

*"To be a person is to have a Story."*

**William. J. Bausch**

#### Setting the conceptual context: Structural Dynamics

We should not underestimate the challenge facing us here as we set out to explore the largely unchartered territory of childhood story. Decades of taboos around emotional vulnerability in leadership positions has left most of us bereft of a way to even discuss the topic. However, the ground-breaking contributions of Kantor's theory and practice of Structural Dynamics enable us to address crucial issues in our society, such as:

- The prevalent myth that we all think, feel and function essentially alike.

- The taboo of pointing out the often vast differences in our inner workings.

- The absence of a common language to address these differences in a value-free way.

Structural Dynamics theory and practice sets out to change two core features of communication. Firstly, faulty communication structures, which we are usually shockingly unaware of, because of the lack of an explicit theory that explains them. And secondly, the Stories in which these communication structures are embedded. The majority of these Stories are typically impacted by sadness, disappointment, anger, or conflict.

## What is 'communication structure'?

When we talk about communication structure in Structural Dynamics we are referring to the three levels of behavioural propensities [our preferences in how we speak and act] that are fundamental to every interaction in all types of human systems [Kantor 2012]. These are as follows:

### Level 1: Action Propensities

The Action Propensities are the behaviours you represent vocally when you are interacting with others. In any effective dialogue, there are four vocal actions, which should be present. A 'Move' sets forth a direction. A 'Follow' validates and completes an action. An 'Oppose' challenges and corrects the action, and a 'Bystand' provides a perspective on the overall interaction and attempts to reconcile competing actions. For example:

**Tony:**  Let's go to the Seaside Café for dinner tonight, I love it there. [Move]

**Sarah:**  I really don't want to go there again! We've been there three times already this month. [Oppose]

**Tony:**  But I really want to go there, it's my favourite place to eat. [Re-stating original Move]

**Sarah:**  We are disagreeing again about where to go for dinner, I wonder, could there be a way for us to find a compromise? [Bystand]

**Tony:**  How about we go there tonight but we go to the new restaurant that's opening in town on Thursday night? [New Move]

**Sarah:**  Sounds great, I'd love that . . . [Follow]

While different combinations and sequences of these actions repeat during conversations, individuals with their own idiosyncratic patterns often gravitate towards some more than others [hence the notion of propensities]. However, where any two or more vocal acts in sequence appear repeatedly, for example, if Tony kept making Moves [setting the direction] and I always Opposed [offered correction], we would have created a structure or pattern, which others would see and experience and which over time could lead to significant frustration and dysfunction. We might also get so used to communicating in this way that we would no longer have any insight into the impact this structure had on others or on ourselves. To help us change the structure, we would need someone to Bystand [provide perspective] about what they were seeing and experiencing or we would need to learn how to be able to do that for ourselves. By bringing in the Bystand and adding in some Follow [offering support and completion] we would be changing the stuck structure and pattern of Move-Oppose-Move-Oppose and as a result be more effective in the interactions between us.

## Level 2: Operating Systems

Operating Systems represent our mindset and characteristic approach to interpersonal interactions; the paradigms that dictate how we navigate the world, including the rules that govern our behaviour and our preferences around the kind of processes we prefer in our communication with others. They originate from our first experience of a system – in our families – and we carry them with us throughout our adult lives. There are three different Operating Systems in which language can be embedded.

'Closed' describes the system in which a great value is placed on tradition, hierarchy and control. It is stable and structured. There are clearly defined roles and processes for doing things. Important decisions are made by the formal, hierarchical leaders.

'Open' prioritises democracy and participation. There is an abundance of teamwork with decisions made by consensus or with the most amount of input possible from the whole team. Maximising the contribution from individuals is paramount in an Open Operating System.

'Random' values creativity unconstrained by formal structures. There are few standard procedures and processes. Decisions tend to be made by one or two individuals who are attending to the particular issue. At its best, a Random Operating System leads to rapid innovation through new thinking.

## Level 3: Communication Domains

The Communication Domains are the three different 'languages', or dialects that people use in interactions. The language of 'Power' puts a premium focus on action and getting things done ["I am reading this book because I believe it will give me the skills I need to help me progress my coaching practice with leaders"]. 'Affect' is the language of relationships, connection and feelings ["I am reading this book because I really care about the leaders I work with and want to maximise the depth and quality of those relationships"], while 'Meaning' is the language of ideas, values and understanding ["I am reading this book because I want to expand and deepen my knowledge and understanding of this model so that I can integrate it into my existing coaching practice"].

In any human interaction, one of the four speech-acts from the Action Propensities [Move, Follow, Oppose, Bystand] and one of the dialects from the Communication Domains work in concert with one of the three Operating Systems, to form one of 36 vocal acts with a distinct structure [like a 'Move in Closed Power' e.g., "I am clear about the need to get this work completed and now you need to get on with it so that you meet the agreed deadline." or a 'Bystand in Open Affect' e.g., "I hesitate to say this but I will, I notice that when the CEO expresses appreciation for us and approves our methods and our outcomes, we all feel really cared for and become even more productive."].

Structural Dynamics is morally neutral in the way that it names and works with these structures in communication. There is no better or worse, there is only 'different'. This enables Structural Dynamics to offer another aspect than the usual 'moral' interpretation of interactions, namely a value-free 'structural' analysis of what is happening in the room. That analysis enables us to reframe whatever tension is playing out in interactions as a conflict of ineffective, mismatching and involuntary patterns [a model clash], rather than a conflict of egos or personalities.

From this base, an experienced Structural Dynamics interventionist can assess what part of the action is getting stirred up and surfaced from the past, and what is actually happening today. As a result, it becomes possible to change the very nature of the discourse from a 'moral' one about right or wrong, to a 'structural' one about natural and justifiable differences in emphasis or approach, and thereby enable more powerful and productive outcomes in our interactions with one another. To be able to phrase an emotion-laden high stakes 'moral story' instead as a morally neutral 'structural story' is also crucial for uncovering the impact of childhood stories in the room.

Everyone has triggers that can put them into high stakes in an instant and without warning. Becoming aware of ones' own childhood story, and understanding it in Structural Dynamics terms is the crucial step in making it accessible as a conscious tool for unravelling the high stakes dramas we find ourselves in. The ugly alternative is being exposed to childhood story as a subconscious force that causes havoc and therefore leads to even more drama occurring in the human/social systems we live and work in. Knowing and understanding one's childhood story makes it possible to notice when it enters the room, to observe and reflect how it contributes to one's own dynamics and dysfunctional interactions, and to free oneself from the dictate of old [involuntary] patterns and emotions. Achieving such a command of their childhood story presents leaders and their coaches with a taxing challenge and at the same time with a phenomenal opportunity to be more skilful than might even be imagined by those not yet aware of the 'power of Story'.

## What is Story: Perfect and Imperfect Love?

In David Kantor's [2012] theory of Structural Dynamics, there are two basic childhood stories of love, which we develop as we are growing up. The first is the story of perfect love in which the child comes into the world with the expectation of pure and unconditional love. The parents or caregivers strive to meet the child's every need, and stories abound about the mythic ways in which perfect love are given to the child. The second is the story of imperfect love, which develops over time as a result of – trivial to most severe – experiences of disappointments, fears, betrayals, punishments and abuse. There are innumerable examples such as:

• Not knowing when the next mealtime is going to be.

• Being yelled at repeatedly for being late or for not doing something you were asked to do by your parent or teacher.

• Being forced to eat food you hated.

• Trying to get your voice heard and being ignored.

• Being consistently hauled up in front of the class to demonstrate something you could not do such as a maths equation.

The list is endless!

The story of perfect love is what should enable us to overcome the story of imperfect love, but if we have never experienced perfect love as a child, then everything becomes much more complicated and complex. It is not impossible though, and I am a living testament to that fact. First, the child comes to terms with the imperfect love. For better or worse, they survive the hurt they experience and, because they cannot change anything, survival itself is naturally paramount. The problem is that this hurt stays and even deepens as the child becomes an adult. But then, when the adult could actually do something different, they don't because they become caught in their own subconscious survival patterns.

The story of imperfect love is also marked by a 'void', a missing component, which is the hero who would – if present – change the outcome of the childhood story for the better and make it come out right. This is known as the Adult Hero Myth in Kantor's [2012] model. There are many aspects to the childhood story of imperfect love and the hero story and each of them has its relevance and needs to be attended to. For example, was there real perfect love or was the alleged perfect love more about the individual's wish to have a happy ending? There is also much to explore and say about the original experience of imperfect love [or outright abuse]. When people have the kind of childhood story that I [and many others like me] had, almost universally, the original disappointment reappears in a marriage or other significant relationship with someone whom you believe, or at least hope, to find perfect love with. This includes close working colleagues.

## Working with Stories and structures

These two strands, Stories and the structures embedded in them, actually present themselves superficially as one 'in the room'. An effective interventionist separates them on the Structural Dynamics premise that faulty communication structures become simply a central part of a Story's architecture; and that by improving the former, you can shape the latter toward a new and better ending. In other words, the communication structures are central to how any Story plays out when triggered in the first place. Therefore, if you work to change the structures you will automatically also be working with underlying Stories. Most Structural Dynamics interventions are conducted in this way with a focus on achieving behavioural change. Deeper childhood stories, while not entirely ignored, are seen as secondary to helping an individual develop communicative competency. Much can be achieved through working with communication structure in this way. However, particularly when working with high stakes behaviours and involuntary reactivity, it is necessary to bring out and work explicitly with childhood story as part of a successful intervention. Childhood story is of the utmost significance to our crisis behaviour. Therefore, in high stakes interventions, working with childhood story becomes absolutely vital, if any real change is to be achieved.

When a person asks for help while experiencing high stakes reactions, they most often convey their experience of hostility, regret or a breakdown in their closest relationships. The role of a good intervention in Story-work is to take you as Story-guide inside the Story-sharer's childhood story so that you can begin to guide the person, for example, from distress and cynicism, to a more positive outlook, based on a new-found grasp and – eventually – even active command over the Story's impact.

Not drawing out and not working explicitly with childhood story creates the risk that you solely attend to surface level symptoms, rather than the underlying cause, and therefore at best you can only effect temporary change. At worst, you may inadvertently be creating the illusion that change has taken place, leading to complacency and a perpetuation of harmful behavioural patterns.

What's needed is a process whereby you move your attention and focus from structure to Story, to structure to Story, in sequence and in parallel. This shift may be replicated many times. There is however, still an important part missing from a workable description of Story-work, and that is the part that the 'internal narrative' plays. The concept of internal narrative is an addition to Kantor's original theory that I offer here.

## 'Story' versus 'Internal narrative'

### Story

When I speak of 'Story' with a capital-S, it refers to the childhood story of imperfect love in each of us. The Story itself might consist of a string of episodic experiences throughout childhood, often repetitively and in different permutations. Together, these episodic stories form our overall childhood story, usually containing accounts of loss, distress and unhappiness.

## Internal narrative

Childhood stories of imperfect love are characterised by impactful, emotional recollections of sometimes prevailing and painful feelings and experiences. However, over time the same Stories gradually form the foundations for an accompanying internal narrative that develops implicitly throughout adolescence and into adulthood. For example:

*"People are unreliable, don't trust too easily."*

*"No matter how hard I try to do what I'm asked, it's never good enough."*

*"No-one ever listens to me."*

*"I'm too fussy."*

*"It's dangerous to answer back to anyone in authority."*

*"I'm just a nuisance and no-one cares about me."*

*"If someone threatens me or my family, I need to fight them."*

In other words, as we move towards adulthood that Story of ours, which in itself is immutable, gets integrated into an 'internal narrative of life'. We craft our internal narrative over time mostly subconsciously, in order to keep our self-image coherent and consistent. The mind abhors nothing more than cognitive dissonance and will do its utmost to keep our adult 'Self' in line with our childhood experiences, and the childhood 'Self' which emerged from them. And so the internal narrative we have constructed usually keeps us forcefully and deeply rooted in behavioural patterns of the past, which have long lost their relevance and make no sense in the adult context. Similarly, it is because of the familiarity of the internal narrative and its associated behavioural patterns that we are also easily coaxed into involuntary, almost compulsive behaviours. This is especially the case in high stakes situations because of how escalation occurs in abrupt and dramatic ways. Suddenly the behavioural range we might generally enjoy in low stakes flies out the window and we become confined to all too memorable ways of reacting.

There is a crucial difference between 'Story' and 'Narrative' at the very core of their nature. While the Story is immutable, and cannot be changed in substance, the internal narrative is no such thing. The internal narrative is constructed based on and around our [usually implicit and from a child's perspective] interpretation of the Story. But what was constructed one way, can also be deconstructed and rebuilt again, but this time based on an explicit and adult interpretation of the Story. The fact that you cannot change what happened to you as a child does not mean that you cannot change your interpretation and perspective of that experience. And that opens the liberating possibility of taking charge and building your own new explicit internal narrative, one which puts you firmly in charge of how you want to make sense of the past and build your future.

## Seeking redemption, saving the child

Seeking redemption and saving the child from the childhood story happens when we go beyond or do something – like Story-work – to get beyond matters in our personal histories that continue to horrify, scare or disable us in our daily lives. Redemption is a transformation where negative aspects of the Self that have been deeply ingrained in our experience are turned into something truly positive that serves us well. Such a transformation involving the redemption of the inner child can be achieved by changing the nature of our internal narrative, but also by adjusting the structure of our behaviour with different kinds of people. The relationship between changing the internal narrative and changing the structure of our behaviour is not necessarily always a linear-causal one. Changing the internal narrative should lead to desirable changes in behaviour, but it doesn't always do so, at least not instantly. It can be an annoyingly iterative process which repeatedly loops back into decidedly undesirable behaviour. However, it can equally be that a half-conscious change in behaviour precedes and informs the conscious writing of a new internal narrative.

Whatever specific path we take, redemption insists that we begin to transform negative aspects of our identity. Having the Self redeemed is critical for being able to write a new internal narrative. Not finding redemption through a new affirmative, enlivening internal narrative means that we will in all likelihood keep repeating the dysfunctional old internal narrative over and over in our adult lives. A dysfunctional old narrative leads to experiences that are like negative residuals that perpetually and relentlessly impact on us. We keep encountering the suffering from our past. The wisdom of doing Story-work is to get beyond those past sufferings, to truly transcend them, so they cannot even haunt us anymore. We know they are there. We notice them, but they have lost their power over us. This is true transcendence. This is possible when we can put our past experiences in a new perspective, in a perspective of the adult who is more empowered and stronger than the child ever was or could have been. So you don't run from the past, you don't fight the past, you don't endorse or comply with the past. You simply reinterpret the past through Bystanding [perceiving, knowing the Story and being aware] as an adult.

## Story-work and the battles that can ensue

With Story-work of the kind advocated here, we are trying to take charge of the internal narrative and change it eventually, rather than live with what has been handed down to us by our childhood subconscious. There is a threshold to cross when you strive to enable a new command of the childhood story, and it takes significant work on the internal narrative to be able to do this. The work of the Story-sharer is first to surface all the different elements of their childhood story and then to become the author of their new, reconstructed internal narrative. A narrative which now contains a different and more desirable range of outcomes, as well as a fresh and enlivening interpretation of the childhood story. This then allows for a coherent integration of the old painful, yet immutable Story, into a new positive and life-supporting internal narrative. It can be hard to imagine a different outcome for the engrained internal narrative at the outset, given that we have to keep working with the old Story as a continued major input, but it truly can be done.

The impact of the childhood story can be so present and powerful that the Story-sharer does not want to change it; they hold on to it with tenacity and can put up a huge fight with you, their Story-guide, when you come to the point of suggesting that there could be a different outcome. Perverse though it may sound, the Story-sharer can be terrified or angry at the prospect of giving up their childhood story of imperfect love. However dysfunctional and painful the impact of the Story might be in practice for them, the thought of changing it can create real anxiety. It can be so hard to believe the very idea that it is possible to take the internal narrative into a different, desirable and actively chosen direction. With the anxiety and disbelief come strong reactions, often as a form of absolute resistance. [You can read more about this in Chapters 7, 8 and 9]. Such resistance is particularly likely if the Story-sharer has not been able to gain a solid grasp of the conceptual framework underlying the Story-work. The crucial difference between immutable Story and malleable internal narrative sounds deceptively simple, but can be such an alien notion while we are [still] stuck in the unyielding trap of our past. It is therefore advisable to combine some theoretical 'teaching of the possibility' to change your old internal narrative with the actual practical 'exploring of that possibility'.

We usually find certain characteristics and ways of being that have dominated – often unhelpfully – in the lives of Story-sharers. It is important to honour those old wounds, but the more exciting aspect that will start to emerge from the Story-work, is about gaining a richer, deeper and more nuanced capacity to understand what is going on in high stakes situations. The Story-sharer can then develop the capacity to act on what they notice in new ways, freed of involuntary patterns dictated by the past. And this is what the·work is all about; to do practical good for people in areas they need help with and to do this by equipping them with the skills to see and notice more, together with a broad and flexible range of appropriate behavioural responses.

Once these new skills and insights are in place, the real talent and mastery so far hidden under the old internal narrative begins to fully emerge. Then – and only then – it becomes possible to begin writing the new internal narrative. The person essentially needs to first expand their powers to see with clarity and act with intent.

> I noticed the presence of my childhood story being in the room as a leader whenever my listening started to diminish, my heart rate rose and I would stop enquiring. I would slip into defending my opinion and not noticing what was happening in the physiology of others. I became stuck driving the direction of the conversation towards action, shutting down dialogue to move through the scenario and to get out of there! I have learned how to do a Bystand on Self when I notice the stakes rising for me. It's so important to be aware of not only the Story but the actual triggers that result in the Story showing up in the room and being able to catch them before reacting to them. My leadership changed immediately through doing this work. Initially I was just less aggressive in my direction setting [making fewer Moves] I noticed more

*and articulated what I was noticing in myself and others
[Bystanding more]. I was less inclined to go straight to
offering correction [not being so stuck in the use of the
Oppose] and was generally more able to draw on all
four of the action propensities [Move, Follow, Oppose
and Bystand]. I also freed myself up to show what I
feel rather than keeping it inside [communicating
more in Affect].*

**Aidan, General Manager**

## Story pathways

Our memory is a complex interweaving of multiple neural connections
that cross, twist and turn. Once established, these connections are akin
to pathways, which become so familiar and well-worn that we become
habituated to them. In turn, thoughts traverse the pathways almost
autonomically and, contained deep within them, reside the tales we tell
about ourselves, the narrative structures and the automatic patterning of
our experiences – our whole lives – which are condensed into schemata.
Our childhood stories are entrenched in these pathways to the extent
that some are so familiar they surface with alarming regularity and
speed. They are never more present than when high stakes triggers take
us to the shadow realms of our behaviour – our worst Self – where, as
the shadows rear up, they distort reality. Yet the same childhood stories
can also account for aspects of our best Self that comes forth when we
exhibit our most shining characteristics.

## Childhood stories

There are many different childhood stories that manifest in complex
and intertwined ways. It would be artificial and limiting to try to create
a definitive typology of what might be seen when embarking on Story-
work. It is also not possible to determine the extent or nature of the
specific impact that will be felt by adult individuals from what might
appear – on the surface at least – to be similar childhood experiences.
Equally, some of the impact we might see, may emanate from childhood
stories that are pre-memory[6], such as the way the person was held when
they were a baby. Or, the experiences themselves may be buried deep
within the recesses of the person's memory – temporarily inaccessible

---

6 We know, for example, from the field of interpersonal neurobiology about the
importance of the first 12 months after birth from which we have no conscious
memory, but are still hugely affected, if not shaped.

to the conscious mind – in part, because of the traumatic nature of them. It could also be misleading to assume that even the most severe abuse leads to a predetermined kind of impact. By the same token, the felt sense from seemingly small moments of loss, disappointment or missed opportunities can echo long and impact in all kinds of ways that can be confusing or might seem incommensurate to the objective experience. One thing that is certain though; the impact of the childhood story, however it has manifested or impacted, will show up in moments of stress or high stakes.

> I would say my experience of my own high stakes responses has often been connected with a childhood story, and one that I couldn't really interpret until recently. I knew there was an innate response, almost an uncontrollable emotional response to something that was happening and tipping me into high stakes when my automatic response would be to want to get away from what was happening as quickly as I could and I would then try to avoid similar situations in the future.
>
> **Samantha, Leader**

With the above provisos in mind, there are some familiar childhood stories that seem to show up repeatedly in Story-work with leaders. Below are a number of common Story-archetypes, along with an illustration of how the child's voice might manifest itself and carry on into adulthood. I offer these as a frame for future reference and further exploration.

## The Injured Child

Children who have experienced physical, emotional or psychological abuse. There is an acute sensitivity to abuses of power, which can result in them putting themselves in harm's way to protect others who they perceive to be vulnerable. They may also strive to occupy positions of power or bypass hierarchical environments to avoid being in a position where they are vulnerable to an unfavourable power differential.

The voice of the child that lives on in the adult: *"Don't hurt me."*

## The Star Child

Children who have been idolised and who go on to idolise others. These children are elevated and celebrated in their family environment, regardless of what they achieve. This Story can lead the adult to connect with a sense of 'love' through idolisation. They seek others who can feed this need because it makes them feel worthy, valuable and loved. There can be an unquenchable desire to seek repeated praise and a sense of dissatisfaction if they are not overtly noticed.

The voice of the child that lives on in the adult: *"Notice me!"*

## The Compliant Child

Children who are made to conform, to follow the rules, to be compliant, to be a 'good girl' or 'good boy'. There is a sense that love is attached to their ability to thrive in a regulated environment which can feel restrictive. This Story can lead to a desire to explore and fully understand the rules of each environment they are placed in. Environments without rules/regulation can seem liberating but also potentially unsafe or confusing.

The voice of the child that lives on in the adult: *"I can't be what everyone wants me to be all of the time."*

## The Carer Child

Children who have lost a parent at an early age, or who have been required to look after their parents' mood, for example, permanently being required to be happy so that the parent can ward off their own depression. Also includes children who have provided physical care for a parent. There can be a tendency for the adult to constantly attend to others' needs at the expense of their own. It can be almost impossible to put themselves first. They can literally wear themselves out thinking and worrying about others with little or no regard to their own well-being.

The voice of the child that lives on in the adult: *"I want to help but I'm trapped and there's no way out of this…"*

## The Abandoned Child

Children who have experienced abandonment of some kind – either physical or emotional. For example, one or both parent[s] left them, or needed to work so relied on grandparents to care for them. They may have been put up for adoption or placed in care. Alternatively, the parent may not have looked after them or cared for them such that they ended up abandoning themselves and their own self-care, sometimes in service of others at the expense of Self or to avoid focusing on caring for the Self which they don't value – "this Self is clearly not worthy because my parents didn't value me therefore why should I?" There is an early realisation that love is not an everlasting concept. This can lead to difficulties in trusting that enduring relationships are possible – believing instead that repeated abandonment is inevitable.

The voice of the child that lives on in the adult: *"Even the people who love me, leave in the end."*

### The Unfairly-Accused Child

Children who have been blamed for things they didn't do or could never have done. There is an imbalance of punishment or the punishment they received outweighed the 'crime' because of a lack of enquiry about what actually happened and resulted in the punishment being unjustified. There is an imbalance of power between the adult and child, combined with a sense of injustice and often the child is silenced. This can lead to sensitivity about equality, fairness and having a voice. The adult may also place a strong emphasis on the importance of enquiry, as a form of compensation for what was not afforded to the child.

The voice of the child that lives on in the adult: *"Please stop blaming me… it's not my fault."*

### The Try-Harder Child

Personified by obedience and dedication to strive for perfection, for success. Failure is simply not an option. The child's environment is characterised by repeated critique of what he or she achieves. No matter what the child did, it was never good enough. Consequently, they are always striving and driving themselves harder and harder in the pursuit of excellence and perfection. This can continue into adulthood and may manifest itself in a fear of failure, a desire to constantly avoid it, and an inability to maintain perspective when failure looms. The adult may be intensely self-critical and intolerant of failure in others. Repeated success at avoiding failure may foster the development of an unrealistic belief in their own invincibility.

The voice of the child that lives on in the adult: *"I'm doing my best but I'm scared I'll never be good enough, no matter how hard I try."*

### The Compelled Child

Children who are strongly driven to realise their potential or a particular goal. They have a weight of expectation placed upon their shoulders from an early age. This includes parents saying things like: 'I want you to have a better life than we do, so please work hard'. It may also be relevant for children who have been over-burdened with the weight and responsibility to achieve something not yet achieved within their family – for example a first child to go to university. It may leave the adult with a particular sensitivity to the idea of letting others down. The adult may also go on to have a curious relationship with the concept of working to a vision that is not their own.

The voice of the child that lives on in the adult: *"I'm worried about letting everyone down… I'm doing my best not to."*

### The Over-Protected Child

Children who didn't have the opportunity to develop coping mechanisms and a relationship with anxiety and staying safe because they were over-protected and often shielded from realities around them. This can lead to a heightened sense of risk and a belief that they are inadequately prepared to cope with new or challenging situations that may present themselves. There can be a sensitivity to abandonment and a desire to keep loved ones close.

The voice of the child that lives on in the adult: *"I'm not OK on my own, please don't leave me."*

### The Unrecognised Child

Children whose parents didn't recognise their different natures. For example, children whose emerging sexuality was ignored or who were otherwise different from their siblings' or parents' expectations. These children may be left with strong feelings of being out of place, acutely aware of not fitting in. As an adult, this may lead them to succumb to pressure to conform or, in contrast, become rebellious in order to break out of convention. There may be an underlying fear of being outcast or they may learn to appreciate their difference and celebrate it. For them, love is connected with true acceptance of who they are.

The voice of the child that lives on in the adult: *"That's not me. Why won't you see me for who I am?"*

### The Loved and Respected Child

Children who are loved and respected regardless of what they did such that they are able to really enjoy life and living. They often feel well-equipped to tackle unfairness, absurdity and obliviousness through argument and constructive action. Assumptions should never be made about the experience of the 'loved and respected child' as this experience in itself can also evoke its own childhood story reactivity that requires attention – not least when they are confronted by a very different reality to their own.

The voice of the child that lives on in the adult: *"I feel secure in most situations and I know I'll be alright."*

In my own case, I most strongly identify with the The Injured Child Story which manifests pretty vividly in my behaviour when I am in high stakes. However, the The Abandoned Child Story and The-Unfairly-Accused-Child Story also feature as part of my identity and therefore, they can also become very evident when I am in high stakes. Context plays its part here too and, depending on what the triggers are, they will activate different Story-archetypes. For example, if I experience what I perceive to be an attack on my integrity, the The Unfairly-Accused-Child Story will come vividly to the fore, and I will come out fighting, showing all the signs of a maudlin victim who – left unchecked – is on a sure path towards being vengeful. In these moments, it is the shadow behaviour that is showing itself.

## Shadows and dark side behaviours

The concept of 'shadow' emanates out of propositions made by Sigmund Freud and Carl Jung. It relates to the hidden parts of the Self that embarrass or shame us in some way. These are the darker sides of the Self that we frequently work hard to keep hidden, yet those who live and work with us know only too well.

> *Everyone carries a shadow, and the less it is embodied in the individual's conscious life, the blacker and denser it is. At all counts, it forms an unconscious snag, thwarting our most well-meant intentions.*
>
> **CG Jung**

We all have these shadow behaviours and it is the childhood story that leads to their development. We evolve ways of dealing with the impact of the Story and they become part of how we approach and behave in close relationships later as adults. Shadow behaviour emanating from the childhood story will always show up in our relationships with others. Childhood stories of imperfect love frequently throw dark shadows on the relationships and get in the way, no matter how hard we try to ensure this does not happen. The Story taints the relationship in some way. This is not only dysfunctional, but also profoundly sad on a human level, and should be a powerful rationale for all of us to do the work necessary to gain command of the childhood story by writing a new internal narrative. This work begins with really getting to know and understand one's own shadows, their source deep in our past, and what triggers them in us now. Ann's experience of working with her shadow behaviours as part of childhood story work she did in her leadership role illustrates this well:

> I found the shadow work both confronting and a relief. Confronting in that I found it challenging to acknowledge my role in things that had upset me. Once I did it, once I was able to go, 'Yes. That is a response I will often have or a trigger or a technique that I will use that I'm not proud of, I'm ashamed of,' in unpacking that, I was able to go, 'OK well there's an understanding as to why that shadow behaviour comes up, but I don't need to do it anymore.' That's where the relief started to come from. I could understand it, and I could see where it came from, and it was not going to go away in its entirety, but it would ebb, and it definitely has done so. It's just taking a breath, observing my ego, myself, and the situation.

> Also, one of the great things Sarah taught me was to just try and separate the elements of what you're actually talking about, lowering the stakes. I constantly find myself thinking, 'Is there a way I could lower the stakes because they seem to get really high really quickly.' It is a relief to acknowledge your own shadow behaviours. Once you notice, name and acknowledge them you can start to do something about them. Most of us deep, deep down don't like those dark responses we have to things, even though we can rationalise them in certain situations. I just got to the point where I thought, 'Well I don't want to live my life like this. It's my life, I don't like relating to people in this way.' You won't get on with everybody, but, fundamentally, I like to relate. I like to relate to people and leave space and room for what they need as well. Is there

*a way to achieve that in this difficult profession I've chosen to be part of? Yes, there is!*

**Ann, Director**

Shadow behaviour is as relevant in private relationships like marriage, as it is at work. In most personal relationships, there is no stopping the shadow, which gradually contaminates the relationship and ultimately breaks couples up, if the behaviours are not dealt with adequately. It becomes possible to extrapolate from the intimate couple relationship to those of a professional kind. How many times have you found yourself in a form of 'break up' with a colleague? A situation where you feel that a bottom line has been crossed, and therefore you have decided to no longer invest in the relationship, or have even made the decision to leave the job or fire the person, if you are in a position of power over them. This kind of thing happens in many work-places, sometimes repeatedly.

Kantor's [2012] heroic modes, Protector, Fixer and Survivor can be helpful in explaining this behaviour. In his original works, Carl Jung conceptualized many different hero archetypes; each has a light and shadow side. In the light zone in Kantor's model, the Protectors will do everything possible to shield themselves and others from harm. The Fixers will set out to conquer all enemies and overcome adversity at all cost, and the Survivors will endure in extraordinary ways, because of their dedication to a cause and focus on getting through oppression and aggression. But in the shadow zone, the Fixer can become aggressive and abusive, the Protector a vengeful maudlin victim whilst the Survivor withdraws or abandons.'

The dangerous shadow side instinctively comes to the fore when subconscious – and often seemingly innocuous – triggers open up an involuntary pathway to past experiences and associated thoughts and emotions. The salutary hero on the other hand shows itself when a justified alarm is set off, when there is real danger in the situation. When the hero comes forward more and more, instead of the shadow, this is usually a sure sign that a new affirmative internal narrative is being written by the protagonist.

## Conceptual framework for Story-work

*A summary*

- There is an immutable childhood story that embodies the child's actual experiences.

- There is an [old] internal narrative that arises out of the childhood story [of imperfect love] and can wreak havoc to the Self and others particularly in high stakes contexts.

- The work to do is to change the old internal narrative.

- The way to do that is through Story-work that enables the Story-sharer to write a new internal narrative.

- In doing this, the person takes command of the internal narrative such that the childhood story no longer has the power to derail and sabotage them in their current situation.

- Remember, it is the internal narrative that changes, not the original childhood story.

- By changing the old internal narrative, the person robs the childhood story of its negative power, redeems the inner child and thereby finds a new kind of confidence, peace and ease in dealing with situations that previously evoked a high stakes reaction in them.

- Know that this is not a linear process. It is highly dynamic and iterative. Story-work requires the Story-guide and Story-sharer to loop backwards and forwards repeatedly.

# Chapter 3

## Enter The Terrain

### Invisible realities, inconvenient truths and other themes

*"That hurt we embrace becomes joy.*
*Call it to your arms where it can change."*

**Rumi**

## Invisible realities

Often we don't have any real clue about the impact that experiences from childhood and adolescence have on us and others. They are hidden in the shadows of our past, and generally we do not even give them a passing thought. We drive onwards and forwards in an effort to live our lives to the fullest as best we can, to survive what went before, to rectify previous injustices, or to simply strive to be the best parent, friend, lover, leader we can be. There is a deep subconscious force that seems to propel us forwards, even if it leads to dysfunctional involuntary behaviour arising out of experiences buried in the past. This can happen to us without warning and, as we saw in the opening scenario in Chapter 1, it often transpires at the most inappropriate of times.

> *Sometimes it's the seemingly simple things that can catch us out as leaders. I remember one occasion as the most senior leader presenting to the Board the strategic plan and the support they could provide. As I was in full flow one of the members looked at their watch and in my mind exhibited a face of disinterest and boredom. As I sarcastically asked them if they had somewhere more important to be than engaged on the future of our organisation, little did they know my childhood story had caught me out; I was about to wreak havoc in my*

*relationship with the Board – some leader! What they
didn't know – and neither did I – until later was that I
had a strong childhood story about being ignored that
regularly impacted on my leadership. The little boy who
felt an irrelevance in his family system with a father, who
always said 'in a minute we'll do this' and never did, had
suddenly made an appearance in the Boardroom. Only
now I had power, intellect and a sarcastic turn of phrase to
punish others with!*

**John, CEO**

My own experience was similar. I can still vividly recall the first time I
realised I needed help with my Story. I found myself 'caught out' as a
powerful reminder from my past rose up to the surface unexpectedly at
an awkward and most unhelpful time:

*I was doing my PhD conducting quasi-ethnographic,
collaborative research with a group of women offenders
attending a probation service behavioural programme.
Esmé, one of the participants, often sneered at me and
made references to me during group activities as being
one of 'them', in other words, like being one of the
Probation Officers. No matter how many times I explained
why I was there, she thought I was a 'spy' from social
services, someone not to be trusted. There were also
times when she became extremely hostile towards me.*

*Notably, I remember one morning she came into the
room and, unprovoked, began screaming at me. Her
outbursts of aggression were always stimulated by alcohol
abuse and in contrast, when she was alcohol free, Esmé
would talk with me, woman to woman, as we discussed
our thoughts about, and experiences of, friendship and
motherhood. There were several times when she confided
in me as she wept following a beating from her husband
and after one vicious assault during which he had raped
her and broken both her arms. She expressed her shame
at having later been found unconscious, lying in the street,
after three days of binge-drinking. As she recounted yet
another beating from her husband following a visit from
the bailiffs, I tentatively suggested the idea of her seeking*

*help from her probation officer. She hit the roof and flew
into a rage, directed at me. She stood so close that as
she screamed I could feel her breath on my face, drops of
saliva rained down on me like venom. In that moment, I
completely froze. I was terrified. I had no clue what to do.*

*Dealing with aggression in a professional context was
not new for me. I had experienced many encounters
with clients when I had been in other roles. So what was
different about this occasion? For one thing, there was
a degree of role ambiguity for me in that I was there as
a research student with no real agency around making
clinical interventions with the women. However, that
wasn't the whole picture. Something else was getting
triggered. My childhood story was in the room in that
moment with Esmé, and it was almost as though I was
transported back in time to being 10 or 12 years old
and my own mother was attacking me all over again.
Historically, the fear I experienced with my mother was
absolute. Her verbal attacks almost always progressed to
physical violence and did not end well for me. Often, I
would freeze in the face of an impending assault. Other
times I would flee. Rarely would I fight.*

**Sarah, Author**

Kantor's [2014] concept of 'Invisible Realities' is based on the idea that
in every meeting of people who talk with one another with the aim of
achieving a shared aim, multiple realities will impact on the interaction
and its outcome. Two of these realities, which are named by Kantor
and illustrated in an accompanying commentary by Hill [2014], are
acutely pertinent to the focus on Story here: one is called the ostensible
reality; and the other, the invisible reality.

The 'ostensible' reality describes the private nuanced perceptions of
interactions that everyone assumes are visible to all, and experienced
in the same way by all parties. We subconsciously sense that this
isn't really the case but nevertheless get lulled in to the comfort of
the assumptions we make. As a result, the false belief that everyone
is observing the same reality tends to prevail despite how inaccurate
this can be. Underneath the ostensible reality, there is an additional
'invisible' reality. The invisible reality is what is playing out in each

individual's mind while they are concurrently engaging and verbally interacting with each other. Whilst you are aware of the content and nature of the interaction between you; and have varying degrees of awareness of the thoughts and feelings you are experiencing as part of the conversation; you have absolutely no access to the invisible realities of others. Therefore, whatever reality is visible in the room can never be anything but ostensible, unless all people in the room have the awareness and skills to openly address the 'Multiple Realities' challenge.

> I am in no doubt that my question to Esmé triggered an aspect of invisible reality where she was reading something in my behaviour and questions and then attributing a different meaning to it than the one I intended. Helping her to unlock the origins of her invisible reality was, in part, a feature of the programme she was attending. However, what was unexpected was how my own invisible reality got activated as I reacted to her response by freezing.

> My reaction was not overtly harmful to Esmé, because I merely froze, but someone did have to intervene to pull her off me, which may not have been necessary had I been able to respond. I may have been able to intervene in such a way as to lower the stakes for her and myself had my own Story not been triggered in the way it was. The experience had a huge impact on me, because I realised that the outcome could have been different. What if I had reacted out of a different kind of shadow, one which would have made me come out fighting too? What if I had gone on to reject and abandon her or punish her in some way? There are all manner of different disturbing scenarios that could have ensued.

> I was shocked by what got triggered in me as a result of this interaction with Esmé, but I will be forever grateful for it, because it prompted me to reflect deeply on my own involuntary behavioural patterns and seek help. Fortunately, my PhD supervisors didn't hesitate in offering me support. I engaged a counsellor to work with for the duration of my fieldwork, which later took me into even more challenging territory inside a women's prison.

*That early work with the counsellor marked the beginning of my personal work towards transforming an outdated internal narrative, based on a childhood story that had kept a tight grip on me right into adulthood. To free myself from these demons of the past, required me to confront my own often hazardous invisible reality and search its root causes. Only then could I proceed to turn the lessons of my past into a true force for good.*

**Sarah, Author**

## Inconvenient truths

There are many challenges associated with transforming an old and outdated internal narrative emanating from a childhood story. Perhaps the most public of all involves dealing with the appearance of what can be described as 'inconvenient truths' requiring an unimaginable and seemingly intolerable exposure of the Self. Inconvenient truths in this context are the ones that everyone would prefer to remain hidden or unspoken, especially you yourself! But as hard as you try to conceal something, you continue to suffer for fear of it being revealed or voiced. Paradoxically, over time, the act of concealment becomes an effort akin to trying to hold an inflatable beach ball under water; it requires constant attention, and is quite difficult in the first place. If you are fortunate enough, you get tired of the relentless effort and eventually let go.

The alternative to letting go and allowing the ball to come to the surface is the risk of exhausting and consequently drowning yourself in your attempt to conceal. This sets the context for Story-work and why it is so imperative. Why risk drowning when you can simply rise to the surface and swim freely like never before, unencumbered by pointless exertions? It is liberating when you stop hiding or denying things you want to conceal. The most powerful and effective people, Story-sharers and Story-guides alike, are the ones who are willing to look at, take in and voice what they have been suppressing or concealing. This is when Story-work comes into its own.

## Critical themes in Story-work

There are a number of critical themes in Story-work that provide a useful contextual frame for the Story-guide to hold at the forefront of their awareness as they contemplate this work with any leader.

## Children experience imperfect love everyday

A child's experience of imperfect love manifests every day, from not being allowed to stay up late, to feeling forced to do homework when they don't want to, to longing for a parent to play with them. At its most extreme, despite all efforts made in our society to safeguard children from harm, family members, teachers, social workers, police and others fail children every day, as their experiences of imperfect love turned abusive go unnoticed. At times, the impact of the catalogue of imperfect love experienced by some children over the years threatens to un-do them, if not during childhood, then as adults. Thankfully, the heroic leader that is in each of us can prevail nevertheless, if we begin the work to transform our suffering into learning and personal growth. More than that, the very same story of imperfect love that, unprocessed, wreaks havoc on our lives, can lead to a depth of gratitude previously unimagined, when it is appropriately explored. Only when directly engaging with it do we start realising how our Story has shaped us in powerful ways which carry as much potential for good as for harm. Often it is only then that we register what really was given to us.

## Adults repeat aspects of their childhood story

Whether victim or perpetrator of harm, we all have agency and as an individual we are the only one who can act to bring about change. We call it:

*"Changing the internal narrative or writing a new one."*

For example, there are many people who grow up believing they are worthless and unlovable in some way. This can become an absolute and unquestionable narrative about the [now] adult Self, while it is actually only an old internal narrative from childhood that can, however, plague a person for decades – sometimes a life-time. Much as they may hate the thought and the lived reality of this old internal narrative, or find it hard to accept it, it is them who are allowing their experience to have such a hold over them. Once they start working on their Story themselves, it becomes possible to develop a new sense of responsibility for how they do have a liberating choice in dealing with their past. We are 'hooked' by our old internal narratives into involuntary responses to interior and exterior triggers. However unhelpful, these old internal narratives provide a level of certainty, what we 'know' to be true about ourselves, such that it can seem inconceivable that it would be possible to change them. And for as long as we allow ourselves to be attached to an outdated subconscious construct in this way, we risk being exactly what we often resolutely and courageously fight to avoid, namely a repeat victim of our childhood experiences of imperfect love.

## The childhood story is a constant companion

It is not possible to eradicate or change the childhood story. It embodies our experience and is part of who we are and who we can be, for better or worse. Pushing your Story away is not the answer either, because when we try to do that, guess what? It bounces right back at us or finds a way to reappear through the backdoor. There is also a sense in which we allow some aspects of the childhood story to continue serving a certain purpose for us even in adulthood. All this makes it really hard to let go. We become attached to our past in complex ways that can be hard to grasp and comprehend without help. The mere recognition that there is a difference between your immutable Story and the internal narrative your subconscious constructed for you, can come as a revelation to people, and open the door to deeper engagement with their childhood story. This is understandable; how often have we heard people say that there is no point in engaging with their childhood story; that it is too painful, and they can't change what happened anyway. Only once people realise the power of the internal narrative, and their ability to actively shape a new and better one for themselves, does Story-work start to make sense.

## Blaming others is common

No-one can make another person think, feel or be anything, however much the maudlin victim inside us may want to go down that route. Blaming others is futile, wasteful and a drain of energy. It is also disempowering. People exhaust themselves in the act. It is vital to take on board that each individual is responsible for their own feelings, and individuals have to do their own work on themselves. When they finally realise they are in control of this, it is an incredibly powerful and liberating experience:

> "I can only change me, it is not possible to change another
> person, or to make a person change. The work begins
> right here with me."

## Durable change requires support

The strength and quality of the relationship between Story-sharer and Story-guide is critical. The need for safety, trust, energy and potential is never more evident than when – inevitably – the moment comes in which the basic premise of the relationship comes under challenge by the Story-sharer. In this moment, the quality of the container that has been built between them will be tested.[7] It may even falter completely and fail, regardless of how strong the initial connection and association has been. When this moment arrives – as it surely will – the Story-guide must remain present, strong and steady in holding their ground so that the work may continue. This includes, amongst other things, not being too quick to back off, and not being too quick to conclude the work in the face of the Story-sharer defending themselves using projection or overtly pushing you away when you get close to a critical Story.

## Retrenchment is inevitable [8]

Just when we think we might be done with working on the childhood story, a trigger is likely to take us right back to square one in how we respond to high stakes. This is called retrenchment. The old internal narrative is still alive and well in these moments. We may find ourselves resenting the notion that such retrenchment is a necessary and vital part of the process of change, and that durable change is simply not possible without it. Retrenchment frequently feels like a crisis when it's occurring and we may also feel like a complete failure whilst we are in the midst of it. It so often comes calling just at the very point where we are feeling more in command of the childhood story than ever before, and where we think of ourselves as well advanced into the writing of a new uplifting internal narrative. Broadly, the work to do when it appears is to open your arms to it and embrace it, safe in the knowledge that it is a critically important and necessary part of the process of deep change.

There is a useful analogy between retrenchment and giving up smoking. The more attempts you try to give up, for days, weeks or even months in between bouts of recidivism, the more time you have not actually been

---

7 William Isaacs [1999] defines a 'container' as: "… the conditions under which a rich field for interaction is more likely to appear… [It is]… a vessel, a setting in which the intensities of human activity can safely emerge. The active experience of people listening, respecting one another, suspending their judgement and speaking their own voice are four key aspects of the container for dialogue." [p 368]
8 The term 'retrenchment' is used in this context to describe the inevitable moments when something happens that evokes the childhood story and the Story-sharer slips back into well-known and well-worn behavioural patterns and reactivity.

smoking within those attempts. The trick is not to beat yourself up too much about each failure but to think of them as limited successes. When you can eventually imagine yourself as a non-smoker, that recidivism becomes much less likely, but the stop-start process is more physically helpful than it feels when you are in the midst of a craving.

## Entering the territory of Story-work

The methods employed for doing childhood story work in this context have largely been evolutionary. Until I began working with David Kantor, I had not been trained in any particular approach. This was in large part because context-specific options for training in this field are limited. Choices are few and far between unless we enter the realms of psychotherapy, psychoanalysis or psychodynamic practice. And yet, whilst these skills and trainings are unquestionably helpful to any practitioner in working with Story, there is a difference between therapeutic intervention that requires that kind of specialist training, and the type of intervention work with leaders that we, as coaches and consultants, engage in every day. In our context, we are not asking leaders to engage in therapy with us where the focus would be placed on treating a psychological or behavioural disorder. We are simply asking them to look behind or beneath the behaviours they manifest in their leadership in order for them to develop their awareness, understanding, and command of their more negative behavioural tendencies. We all know that in the absence of such reflection, leaders can easily create mayhem in the room, especially when the stakes are rising for them.

> The childhood story for me was one of listening to my dad talking at me, that was the essence of it. And it resonated significantly with how my CEO was behaving in my conversations with him. He is somebody who tends to spend a lot of time in extended monologue about his view of the world or his kind of experiences as a senior manager. I often found myself in a situation where I would be sitting and listening to him but also thinking about other things rather than having a two-way exchange. It led to being more aware that that's how I experienced those interactions, and that I needed to be much more self-prepared going into them. The work on childhood story helped me to develop two or three simple steps that I could take when I was in meetings with that person or others who behaved in similar ways. So it emerged

*very naturally. It wasn't a particularly painful or awkward situation to engage in. It was a very natural thing to do. Sometimes you do get anxious or you can get anxious about reflecting on these things. But I think what it reminded me was that so much of what we do or how we think and how we behave as adults is framed by personal family experiences which are relatively easy to recall. The issue for me was how prepared I was to honestly reflect on that and bring that into the coaching conversation.*

*What's changed is that I allow conversation to flow a bit more, rather than closing it off. I don't offer up my fixed view on something as early in a conversation, I might still offer up my view, but perhaps offer it as being less fixed. So I offer my opinion as being a significant voice, rather than 'the answer is X if you only just listened to me' type of response. I think in meetings and one-to-ones otherwise I try to get into how people are thinking and feeling rather than just into what they believe. I think these are subtle but quite marked differences. I'm more aware when I'm irritated. I'm more aware of the triggers that trigger me, and I'm also very well aware of when I am triggered to behave in a way that I don't particularly want to behave. I can't always stop it, but I'm more aware of it.*

**Donald, Chief Officer**

Childhood story work is functional and has simplicity to it, but it is also far from intuitive or easy. It needs skilful, confident practice from properly trained Story-guides. However, time and again I have heard identical concerns being expressed by coaches. There appears to be a real nervousness about entering this territory. It might be for fear of being asked to act as therapists without having the necessary training. Fear of professional overreach looms large:

> *"What if the person breaks down? What if I do damage by asking a leader to share their childhood story when I am not a trained therapist?"*

I have even been accused of being irresponsible in suggesting that we as coaches/consultants might do this kind of work with leaders at all.

A real concern seems to exist that it is in some way dangerous. But in reality there is no recklessness in the proposition. On the contrary, as you will read further on, practitioners can potentially do harm by not entering the territory of childhood story with the leaders they engage with, and, of course, by doing so, but without appropriate training. Below Mark talks about this from his perspective as an Organisational Development Consultant and Dan does so from the perspective of having once been a therapist, but now working in the territory of Structural Dynamics and Story-work:

> *People hear 'childhood story' and prickles go down the back of their neck, but some of the best interventions are reasonably simple. I don't want to underplay the work you need to do on Self, and the importance of training to be able to do this work, but it doesn't need to be that daunting either. Don't be afraid! You don't have to be the deepest, most confident psychologist to do this work and give good value from it.*
>
> **Mark, Coach**

> *There can be a big block to openness to this whole area, which I think erupts like a volcano from sceptics and many others, 'That's therapy. We don't go there because – Oh my God, what could happen, if we start talking about this, that or whatever?' Yet I think as society and its communities of leaders, we have just somehow got rid of so much dialogue; Let's talk about the consequences of leaders not expressing when they're vulnerable, not expressing when they need help, not expressing when they're having a bad day. Let's explore health and well-being, let's talk about the consequences of not being able to have deep dialogue with each other. I'll often talk with groups about that and go, 'Tell me the cost of that.' Look at the suicide numbers around the world. The consequences of not being able to be socially resilient through open dialogue where we're deeply listened to and those implicit motivators around, 'I feel valued, listened to and cared for.' We do not tap into these resources and we have people relying on individual resilience to solve deep stuff that we need others' help*

*with. The consequences of not going there are far greater than going there.*

*From my experience as a therapist, I think that the therapeutic world and people operating from that frame are likely to spend more time exploring childhood story and be coming from a frame of the value of somebody's Story being listened to. They work very much on the relational aspects in-the-room and the therapist's experience, the relationship that the person has with the therapist and a belief that the healing and value will be from somebody being heard. There's a lot of emotional processing. In debating some of the traps of therapy, I think therapists can be overly indulgent in reflecting on the past and what I find very purposeful is attending to exploring childhood story from a frame of its impact on the here and now. The transition for me moves from, 'I'm going to listen to this person tell their childhood story and explore it and they'll be better for having told me,' to 'What are the insights and what's the new internal narrative that can be written now?' and 'What's the way the person can lower their stakes from understanding the triggers associated with a childhood story?'*

*I think the experiences people can have of doing Story-work reduces the anxiety so much that they realise there's not a lot they have to do – the capability has always been there to attend to this. What has got in the way is people's anxiety! There is this unhelpful narrative that means capable people go, 'Whoa, I can't go there. Could you imagine what could happen?' I go, 'Gee, it's actually a privilege and an honour and you often don't have to do that much.' I don't want to be reductionist around it and simplify the whole thing, but you know where I'm coming from?*

**Dan, Coach**

## Story-work in coaching: Challenging the stigma of therapy

In presenting Story-work as an approach to employ in coaching, I am not setting out to compete with or critique therapy. Rather, I am offering it as a methodology coaches can use to engage leaders in deep behavioural work on the Self that potentially makes such work more palatable to a leader. The context is the accepted canon that successful executive leaders do not need therapy, or at least they don't admit to needing it. People in leadership positions are in those positions because of their ostensible ability to function. When you are at the top it can be very hard to accept real help in general. "After all, what do we pay you for if you need help in doing what you've been hired for?" But it is particularly hard to even consider that you might need help with something deep down in your 'make-up,' in 'who you are,' and 'how you operate'. That something might need repair, and you might need to do some work to become fully effective. This leads to individuals maybe being willing to talk about getting stressed or experiencing 'burn-out', but the notion of admitting to the need for therapy is widely stigmatised as a kind of professional death sentence. Obviously we all know that – objectively – this is crazy, and that many people in business, Government and in public life – especially celebrities – struggle mightily with functioning in the roles they have worked so hard to achieve. But just as we have taboos about speaking openly and pointing out deep behavioural differences in people, we also have taboos about addressing the behavioural dimension of people in high office.

The stigma of not being 'behaviourally healthy' can loom even larger than the penalty for acting out horrible behavioural pathologies, as many leaders unfortunately do. Therefore, those who desperately need input never even get to the starting point, because they simply refuse the notion of engaging with anything even remotely looking like therapy. Only when everything completely breaks down, when a leader's behaviour becomes totally untenable, might there finally be a dramatic change. The leader will either burn-out or be thrown-out and replaced with the next one, who will bring their own pathology of hidden involuntary behavioural patterns; and so, around we go again. This 'throwing out the baby with the bathwater' approach – familiar to anyone who follows Premiership football in the UK and the way managers come and go – is not a healthy way to develop and nourish any team or organisation, and yet it is only too common.

A paradigm shift is needed to break out of this vicious circle. We urgently need to stop oscillating between hero-adulation of leaders on the one hand, and trying to diagnose them as flawed and therefore in need of 'repair' on the other. The former will most likely make them arrogant, the latter they will rightfully resist until their last breath – the result for their organisations is entirely predictable, though: stagnation interspersed with erratic disruptions.

Coaching has generally been marketed as 'everything but therapy'. As coaches, we are working on effectiveness and efficiency, on tools and methods, on freeing the potential of the client, on un-cluttering busy minds, but rarely on the more deeply rooted behavioural short-comings of the powers that be. This 'positioning' of coaching is very smart because with the stigma attached to therapy, it will always be challenging to get [most] leaders to go 'there', even if they are in desperate need of help. Instead, they frequently exhaust themselves, visit havoc on those around them, endanger the survival of their organisations and their closest intimate relationships – everything but admit to the need for therapy.

This is where childhood story work can make a real difference, because of how it provides a non-threatening way to explore deeper forces and shadows in leaders. Story-work lowers the barrier to engage in constructively challenging – albeit potentially painful – reflection about the Self, any associated dysfunctional behavioural patterns, where all this might stem from and what can be done to change those patterns. This is more than 'normal' coaching, but it can be distinctly different from therapy. We might even have the same effects as therapy at the end of successful Story-work, namely that dysfunctional behavioural patterns are altered or eliminated.

In Story-work – in contrast to therapeutic intervention – you do not go back into the depths of the details of events with the purpose of treating a psychological or behavioural disorder. Story-work is about acknowledging the existence of such [dramatic and potentially traumatic] events, naming what they were, exploring them in order to place them in time, as well as understand the impact they had back then and may still be having now. This is followed by going to work on writing the new internal narrative in a way that counteracts old patterns of reactivity, preventing them from having such influence and power. This book introduces practitioners to this vital and demanding work. It does so by taking the reader into the depths of Story-work. We will explore what's involved in guiding leaders in relation to the impact of their childhood stories; and how to do this in an appropriate and competent way through skilful counsel, exploration, support and challenge.

Instead of pointing out that somebody becomes dysfunctional in high stakes, or has a behavioural disorder which shows itself under stress, in this approach, it is understood and expected that under stress [i.e. in high stakes] most of us regress to a degree, show less behavioural flexibility and can even become totally blocked. In such moments leaders should be able simply to ask themselves:

*"Is there any link between stressful events of the past, and my behaviour under stress today?"*

And if the answer is "Yes", as it undoubtedly will be in most cases, they can set to work on exploring this link between past and present and evaluating whether their 'old programming' is still serving them well today. Out of simple questions like these – with the proper guidance of an experienced Story-guide – reflections will usually emerge over time and an eventual re-writing of the internal narrative will be possible. These steps have the potential to profoundly change behaviour and eliminate much involuntary shadow behaviour under stress. The same people who would never entertain the notion of entering therapy, can attain practical results for their professional and private lives which would be considered 'dream outcomes' for any therapeutic intervention, without ever having the feeling that they were undergoing therapy. And that's how it should be.

In summary, Story-work:

- offers a unique chance to bring profound support to where it's needed most, to people who influence the lives of hundreds, thousands and even millions through their roles as leaders.

- provides an alternative for those individuals who urgently need help and support on behavioural matters, but who so far have flatly refused such help.

- has the capacity to reach a segment of people who today are largely left to their own devices, ostensibly out of choice, but in fact due to social pressure.

- makes no pronouncements about therapy; it simply focuses on how to get the necessary help in palatable form to where it is needed the most.

## Combining therapy with Story-work

A leader might, of course, also combine approaches, starting first with Story-work and progressing to some kind of therapeutic intervention, or it might happen the other way around. Here's Ann's account of having first engaged in therapy and later gone on to do Story-work with me in the context of her role as a leader:

> I went to see a therapist at a time of great crisis. I really started working on myself with him. I was very unhappy in my work. I was very conflicted. I had lost a huge amount of confidence. I was thinking of not working again in my field. I remember very clearly the first session because we sat down and he asked me what I was there for. I started to talk about the people I was working with and how I felt about what they had been doing. He said, 'It's very frightening when you get that angry.' I remember thinking, 'Oh my God, you're actually going to make me look at myself. OK, OK!' and I really quickly realised I had gone there for a quick fix and that that might not be possible.

> Then we started working and I'll always love him for that. He was great. But we talked a lot. We did a lot of very, very fundamental work to try and unpack where some of my behaviours had built up from, why I would be triggered or react to certain things in such strong ways. That's when I started going back into childhood story. Then when I came to the UK, I had another period where I was struggling. I spoke to my therapist and he put me in touch with Sarah.

> The work was almost immediately very illuminating and cathartic and ultimately a very peaceful process which was not what I expected when we started. It has been profoundly helpful in my personal and my work relationships. It's been very good to understand what is old, what is of the child and what might be actually of now through trying to observe the Self and take the time to do that. We also talked about the strength of the Bystand and the Follow and how to try and help within a room filled with people who weren't being heard and those kinds of things. I found it a great process; it was very good.

When Sarah first asked me about my childhood story though, I remember it quite clearly because I was thinking, 'I have done that, haven't I?' I've done years of therapy in my life. But Sarah presented it in a very functional, clear way that to me kind of visualising it, I felt like it was a bridge between my two selves. She was the first person that enabled me to think, 'It is worth going back.' I realised what I'd done was to kind of sort and package it and I didn't initially want to look at it again. Actually, what Sarah was doing though was illuminating the fact that it is a huge part of who you are and maybe it's OK to find a way to live with that, look at it, know it, even make friends with it rather than feeling you have to unpack all these boxes. Initially she had me just look at the key triggers, the key aspects of what happened and, yes, it was so good. I think as you get older you can often assume that that was what happened then or you know everyone has bad childhoods. It's difficult, it's hard.

I think the main difference I noticed about the childhood story work from the therapeutic work I had done was how functional it was. It was almost like Sarah was able to help me break it down into digestible chunks, my childhood; the narrative that I had told about it, and shine small amounts of light on sections so I could absorb it. Earlier therapy seemed to involve a lot of talking and certain responses, but the work wasn't so concrete. I really responded to the pragmatic way of sitting back, looking at it, observing it, questioning whether that was, in fact, true; really honestly looking at your adult behaviour in relationship to that childhood story. It was the connective tissue between the two that really, really helped me. It really brought a lot of peace with my relationship with my parents in a fantastic way because it was OK for it to be whatever it had been. That was alright. It no longer felt like a weight that I had to carry around. The history of what had happened in the family, the fracture of the family, the kind of betrayals and lack of trust and the hurt. There was so much hurt in the family unit for so long. The work that I did with Sarah just seemed to really enable me to let that be and to be very kind to that child and acknowledge *it, rather than examine my role in it or anything. I was able to look at it as a child who didn't need to take responsibility for that, and that was very profound. I'm very grateful for it, really.*

**Ann, Director**

## Story work of the Story-guide and the Story-sharer

As described in Chapter 1 [and developed further in its own chapter, see Chapter 11], the basic assumption is that any coach who wants to do Story-work with their clients, has to first do work on their own childhood story. This is not just for generally improved intervention outcomes, but because it is crucial for the coach to be in command of their Story and its accompanying internal narrative. It is also important for the coach to be able to stay steady, solid and strong in the presence of a likely barrage of trigger events and themes when working with clients. Pressure and perturbance are present both when working with clients in individual coaching, and when working with them in live team-meetings or interventions. Perturbance is such a critical feature of Structural Dynamics intervention [see Chapters 6, 7 & 10 for more information] and the high stakes context leaders operate in is so prevalent, it is likely that the intervention will be intense, and the stakes will easily get high for participants as well as the coach at times. With these contextual factors in view, it has never been more important that coaches have done work on their own Story, their internal narrative and their triggers, before embarking with others on the same. Otherwise the risk is that they will be easily dragged into high stakes reactivity, and instead of helping others to avoid havoc, they might contribute to and fuel it, even if this is the furthest thing from their minds.

A further question is whether there needs to be a clear distinction between the level or degree of work to be done by coaches on themselves [with their own Story-guide], and that of the clients [with the coach as Story-guide]. Are these two distinct types of Story-work, with the coach needing to go deeper than the client? One response could be to highlight a continuum in the intensity and depth of process required between the Story-work done by coaches acting as Story-guides, and that of their clients engaging as Story-sharers. In this scenario, the Story-guide would need to have done the deepest possible work on themselves, if they are to guide others through a similar in-depth process over many months. At the other end of the continuum, as we will see in more detail in Chapter 4, Story-work can take the form of a simple enquiry of a leader: asking them to notice, name and acknowledge their childhood story and the impact it is having in their everyday leadership. This is not difficult to do, and as such, one could question whether intervention at this level requires the same depth of personal work on the part of the coach. However, on balance I think that it does. Story-work is not formulaic. The coach needs to be able to assess when to pause, when to proceed, when to dig deeper or when to ease back. To do this they need to know their own invisible reality, how it manifests, and how it even contributes to these choices. Story-guides need to be able to work with their own internal narrative, so that they are confident about being able to:

- Dare to 'ask' [others]

- Help others dare to 'look' [at themselves and their Story].

# PART TWO

*Tread The Winding Path*

# Chapter 4

## Dare To Ask, Dare To Look

### Beginning the work

*"What is the source of our first suffering?
It lies in the fact that we hesitated to speak.
It was born in the moment when we
accumulated silent things within us."*

**Gaston Bachelard**

**Dare to ask**

In Story-work, a key premise is that the very process of daring to ask about and uncover childhood stories already reveals a lot about the causes of dysfunctional behavioural patterns. This revealing is, in itself, already curative. Story-sharers must see any mess or confusion for what it is, before they can even try to clean it up. They have to identify any barriers and figure out how to get through them.

> *I had failed to feel any compassion for myself in relation
> to what happened to me growing up. I needed to go
> back there to uncover and share what happened in order
> to begin to do that. In doing so, I could heal the wound I
> had carried around with me for decades.*
>
> **Sarah, Author**

Addressing the concern mentioned earlier, about potentially causing harm through eliciting a childhood story – it is important to know that even expressions of emotional trauma are not necessarily harmful if the Story-guide provides sufficient levels of support and suitable guidance. Throughout more than two decades of working with clients in various roles as a social worker, researcher, dialogue facilitator, coach, interventionist and Story-guide, the people I have worked with have consistently demonstrated outstanding strength, depth of feeling and often urgent desire for their Stories to be heard and understood. Whilst it has, of course, not always been easy territory to enter, their feedback has consistently been that the experience has been liberating. In large part, this was because the Story-guidance allowed them to face their own limits and internal conflicts, and then set out to work on these, especially on the darker, more shadow-ridden aspects of their behaviour that had previously been largely invisible to them. Until I asked about their childhood story, no-one had seen the purpose of inquiring into what was behind their high stakes behaviour, and no-one had been curious to explore with them what might be lurking there. The endeavour in Story-work is to bear witness to individual's voices, to bring an end to their silence, to have their Stories heard, and to set free the transformative potential that is in all of us, if we only dare to really go there.

> As a leader, I had told and retold my childhood story
> in many different situations to send out a message
> of resilience, calm thinking in a crisis and an ability to
> stand on my own two feet. The abandoned child was
> dependable because they had been abandoned. Only
> when asked to tell the Story in the coaching relationship
> did I see behind the light side Story I peddled with
> aplomb and which had served me well in getting into the
> top echelons of public life, to a darker Story which was
> about my own serial abandoning of others and systems.
> The abandoned child knew how to abandon others with
> ease!! I needed to explore this Story, because this is what
> was showing up in the high stakes context I was operating
> in and at times was threatening to derail me.
>
> **John, CEO**

Practitioners might have understandable concern about inadvertently causing harm when daring to enter Story-territory with leaders. Might asking even one question about a leader's Story already be going too far? And yet, in my experience, nobody has ever been harmed as a result of sharing their Stories. In dozens of interventions, nobody ever said that actual damage was done. Also, what exactly does 'going too far' mean? I hear coaches and interventionists express this apprehension a lot. We might think we are stating our concern for the client, but there may be something else happening here – namely our own fears of the Story and its expression by the Story-sharer. This may stem from the Story being in some way distressing to us as coaches, or we may be connecting to something in our own Story. My heart was beating at about 160 beats per minute the first time I asked a CEO about his childhood story, right after coming out of a situation where he had shown all the signs of not being in command of his behavioural patterns.

I candidly admit that at times I felt overwhelmed by the depth and power of some Stories. Yet I have never regretted listening to and staying with the Story-sharer, and helping them find their own way of laying their Story to rest. The reluctance to ask a question about childhood story might actually say more about the coach, their invisible reality and their own behavioural preferences, than reflecting the needs of the client. An example of this could be; if I as the coach am someone who is high in Closed Power [disposed towards structure and efficacy and speaking primarily in the language of action], combined with a disinclination towards expressions of Open Affect [i.e. not someone who is leaning towards connecting in relationship and speaking in the language of feelings], I may not be so comfortable with doing deep childhood story work on myself and with others, or I may not see the relevance of it.

Linked to this might also be a practitioner's fear of being fully able to hear, bear witness to, or simply be with someone, when they catch sight of a significant Story from their past. There can be something unsettling in being next to a person who begins to see how their Story might have shaped the way they handle themselves in their relationships, and the [negative] impact this had on others. This uneasiness about Story is only too understandable. In a sense, it reflects the very essence of Story itself which discourages and inhibits us from exploring our full potential. It does this not only through evoking involuntary behavioural patterns, but by protecting itself from being discovered as the very source of such troubles. That's an amazing defence mechanism which can easily keep us from even trying to get close to it, and then the old Story can continue to do its damaging work unperturbed. We should not allow this to happen, but to enter into 'Story-territory' we need to keep in mind that proper training and ongoing support in the form of supervision[9] is crucially important.

---

9 'Supervision' in this context refers to the relationship with a professional supervisor [Experienced Story-guide] whose aim is to enhance the professional skills, growth and experience of the supervisee [Story-guide] with the aim of ensuring improved outcomes for the clients [Story-sharers].

## Courage and challenge

There is no doubt that it takes courage to explore a childhood story, no matter how big or small, seemingly trivial, or deeply profound that Story is. But what does it even look like, and what needs to be attended to when challenging coaches and interventionists to dare to enquire into their own or another's childhood story? In daring to ask questions about the past it is important that the enquiry is relevant and in response to something you are noticing in either the structure or Story you are working on with the person right now. It should be the most natural thing in the world to 'go there'. We need to be careful not to enquire into childhood story for the sake of it, or simply by rote. Below Donald describes his experience of this when he and I were working together in a coaching relationship:

> *Sarah asked me to do a bit of work, to maybe just think about where I thought in my childhood experiences that a particular behaviour she had witnessed may have emerged from. It was a very natural part of the conversation, it wasn't a, 'Right, let's now talk about what happened to you in childhood, and can you go away and think of a childhood story that might influence your day-to-day behaviour?' It was very much contextualised by the coaching experience and interaction within that. So I didn't have an adverse reaction to being asked about my childhood story because it denoted very naturally. At its simplest, Sarah was describing how many of one's behaviours are framed by these kinds of childhood experiences, and did I think that might be the case, and did I want to spend some time reflecting on that, bringing that back into the next coaching session – which is what I did. I didn't find that particularly hard to do because it was very relevant to the context in which I was being coached in that sense. We didn't start the coaching conversation by Sarah giving me a lecture on adult behaviour being framed by childhood experiences, then randomly having to think about that.*

> **Donald, Chief Officer**

A Story-guide might also ask someone how they learned to behave in a particular way that is distinctly noticeable [at least to others], or enquire about what might be behind a striking behaviour someone is manifesting in their professional relationships. These are relatively straightforward and simple questions to ask, and they can be posed by the Story-guide without concern, safe in the knowledge that it's simply not possible to force someone to answer against their will in a professional coaching relationship, which after all is far from the extremes of interrogation or torture! The Story-sharer will let you know if they are not ready to engage, by simply not answering you, by telling you explicitly to 'back-off', or by overtly expressing their fear or unwillingness to go there. In such moments of overt or covert resistance, the role of the Story-guide is to use the reaction as data and to 'stay with' the person and their Story. Reactions of this kind are valuable feedback that indeed there is a Story there. Simply naming this can often be enough. There is no need to probe further into the actual Story content. Rather, there is now an opportunity to voice your hunch that there is a Story that could be impacting current behavioural patterns in some way, while at the same time stating clearly that you are not going to probe any further into specifics.

> There are some situations where I don't go fully into working on Story, I don't say, 'Let's spend some time on your childhood story', I go gently in. I'll say, 'Seems like this person is getting you pretty stuck, is this behaviour familiar? Does this pattern feel familiar? Have you seen this before? When was the first time you felt this way?' So gentle enquiries into some connection to the past. These kinds of questions allow you to get into Story early in the coaching.
>
> **Bridget, Coach**

This 'light touch' approach allows the Story-sharer to acknowledge the potential existence of a relevant childhood story without being compelled to explicitly talk about it right away. Often it is such acceptance that prompts people to spontaneously want to say more. For others, you might see that they are starting a process of reflection, and therefore return later to the topic. Like with good wine, sometimes a new thought has to age naturally in a client, before it is ready to be consumed publicly.

Having dared to ask the question as a Story-guide, there may also be times when the Story-sharer struggles to connect with a childhood story, finds it really uncomfortable to talk about, or reports that there simply was not a story of imperfect love, that their childhood story was all positive, filled with love and respect.

When I started, I had an absolute belief that my childhood was fine. I really struggled to connect with my own childhood story and when I heard some of the more extreme examples where people shared significant Stories about physical and emotional abuse, and I hadn't had any of those experiences, I really struggled to say, 'You know what? My parents were great.' I have also worked with other people that are like, 'I don't have a negative childhood story.' So yes, absolutely there are people that are like, 'I don't have any negative Stories that have formed how I behave when I am at my worst.' But you know, I've never not got there with the person. It can take some time and even with myself it took time to connect to, really what are the Stories? My Stories aren't horrendous but they don't have to be. They are Stories that may be insignificant to every other person but they had a significant impact on me and still do.

**Mark, Coach**


I remember saying, 'Oh yes this is really great, and I am really enjoying it,' and then on the inside going, 'I am hating it, this is so hard.' I really wrestled with what was coming up for me, that caused me to have a deep response to the things that we were talking about. I remember confessing this and I said, 'But I think I understand the reason why that might be,' so, we had this great conversation. I described how I felt as though I was one of those cupboards that are so full of stuff that you just throw everything in and then shut the door quickly but then you don't want to open the door again because a lot of things are going to tumble out and you're not really sure what that's going to be. And the reason I felt really uncomfortable about even just reaching for the handle to open that door, was that I didn't want to blame my childhood for the things that were coming up for me. Once we'd had that conversation, then it really freed me to go, 'This is not about blaming my past; this is about *just understanding it as really useful information which means that the meaning I have attached to things drive a particular behavioural response in me.' By framing it like that, I can respect and still appreciate and love the people in my childhood story, without being at risk of blaming those that are the closest and most central people to my context. It was an extraordinary thing to experience and then to appreciate saying, 'Yes, of course, there are still some things that are very challenging. But actually, there's a way into understanding that now, which is more about appreciation than anything else and seeking to understand.'*

**Samantha, Leader**

'Sticking with it' and gently exploring further are important in these moments when 'imperfect love' seems too distant or too scary to contemplate for people. You can be sure though, there will be a Story.

It is also right to be concerned about the timing of and approach to opening up a Story-line with someone. To ensure that Story-work is a force for good, we must never be reckless in doing it, and we must always be ready for the unexpected to occur. Both Jack and Mark's experiences 'in the room' illustrate the importance of this:

*Deep in the thick of an intervention with 20 senior leaders from across the organisation, my co-interventionist and I noticed how dismissive and disrespectful the leadership was of the CEO in the room. As I asked the CEO to join me in the centre of the room for a conversation about what it was like being the CEO in this place, little could I have known what would happen next. Within a couple of minutes, the CEO shared her childhood story, made connections between her own behaviours and that Story in-situ and, in so doing, the whole dynamic in the group changed! They said it was as though they were seeing her as human for the very first time.*

**Jack, Coach**

*I was reasonably comfortable with the childhood story being present for the clients I was working with, but then* starting to work with it with them, whilst it was incredibly empowering, I also found it incredibly daunting, just because of the significance and importance of the work and trying to live by a philosophy of doing more good and less harm, of course. It's difficult. I've probably got a unique perspective because I am working as a Structural Dynamics Interventionist within my own organisation so the desire to dare to ask is one thing but the ability to hide behind, 'Is this safe from an HR 'care for people' perspective,' is also there. It does really highlight the importance of contracting and getting that right in building a container and establishing an environment where people within the organisation feel comfortable to go into working on their childhood stories.

The other thing for me when I started doing this work was that I assumed it may have been difficult in terms of getting people to want to go there and see the relevance or the importance in it. But my lived experience of that is completely opposite and there has actually consistently been a strong desire to do so once the individual leader starts to make a connection and talk about some of their behavioural preferences. This is particularly when you start to look at some of the contextual, sub-surface stuff that drives some of the different bad behaviours; people eagerly want to go there.

I can remember one of the early people I worked with in this territory. She was a General Manager, managing the bottom half of the country for the company. We were doing work with her team around the year's strategy and how they came together as a new team along with some challenges they were already facing. I was doing an individual debrief with her using the Kantor Behavioural Profile. The first time she dialled in five minutes late, she was in a cafe, flat out, didn't have the profile with her and so I stopped it. I said, 'We're not going to do it now.' I think that was important in terms of the impact that might have had on the contracting in the container. Then a week later, she had done the pre-work but she dialled in, absolutely in a flap around, 'I know I've got to get this *done but I've got the CEO coming down, all these people have let me down, got all this stuff to do, and so you've probably got half an hour tops with me.' I was like, 'Here's someone completely in high stakes,' it wasn't what I anticipated. It threw me in to my own high stakes because I had a loose plan for the session and then now I had someone who was obviously distracted and it limited my time. That session, because it was so real and she was in it, I could work with her there so it wasn't around, 'reflect on a time when . . .,' or – I wasn't actually having to create the perturbance. I was like, 'This wasn't planned but here we are, she's obviously in high stakes and she wants to connect.' And as we started to get closer in to it she wanted to keep working more deeply with it.*

*That for me was one of my first experiences where I went into childhood story linked to high stakes deeply with an individual. It was a great session. We just went there. I think we ended up spending an hour and forty-five minutes together. She asked for more time with me the very next day despite all the pressures she was experiencing around the CEO visit. It was very valuable work for her and led to real change within that real situation. This was a real, live scenario, so, moments like that present themselves, and again that goes back to you as a practitioner, you can't assume what will come up. And not everything is going to be sign-posted when you start that this is a high stakes intervention, or that this is going to be a high stakes coaching arrangement. Or, 'I'm purely going to keep this at level one.' I think you've got to be prepared to understand that the individual might just go there . . . or not.*

*She put me on the spot and said, 'Can you elicit my childhood story?' It was a bit of an opening, to say, 'I really want to go there.' I also later discovered that this was actually part of her Story, in other words, outsourcing effort around understanding herself and that hard work on Self. I didn't know it at the time but it came out that it was typical behaviour for her. It was like, 'You know what? I'm not going to do the work on myself, you do it for me.'*

*So even that was brilliant learning. But what I was able to do – I didn't try to elicit the Story in any way, we just worked back through the original live example. What was the behaviour she was displaying? What were the specific things people did half an hour ago, today, very recently, that had seen her respond in such a way? And then I worked that back to saying, 'Where have you learned that behaviour? You know, those triggers link to things.' And we started to get into some of the stuff around the relationship with her father. She talked around the young adult hero myth and the esteem with which she held her father. She described how this had influenced the esteem to which she held herself and others and that this was based on the impression, or the image, she held of her father. She talked about how when that was compromised or she sensed someone was letting her down that that's when some of her high stakes behaviours would start to be triggered and she would act out of her shadow.*

*The power of the work I did with her was that she could leave that session understanding what impact she might have been having on others. So she had an increased understanding of, 'Hey, there's this stuff going on here for me that I can control. But also how I've responded is also potentially having an impact on other people.' So from where I thought this session would go, to where she thought the session would go, to where we ended up an hour and a half later was really incredible. I guess the summation here is I should not have made any assumptions around people's willingness to go there, and the benefit they get from even a light touch of daring to ask the question. It's not always easy but lean in, have the courage, have the vulnerability, lean in to the Story, so much good can come of you doing that.*

**Mark, Coach**

While you do need to 'dare' to ask, recognising your limitations as a Story-guide is equally important. So how do you 'know' where to step forward or to draw back when pursuing the recollection of the Story? As the remaining chapters of the book unfold, I will introduce the principles and practice guidelines for making these decisions and for embarking on the journey of Story-work. But first, let's explore what it takes for a Story-sharer to dare to look at their childhood story.

## Helping the Story-sharer 'dare to look'

Our childhood story is special to us, because it is ours and – as we will see more fully later – it is linked to our identity. Absolutely everyone has a childhood story. We also have a tendency to make our own internal narrative – emanating from that Story – so big and give it such power that it can continue to do us damage all through adulthood. The childhood story is actually embodied in our actions, and through these actions it also impacts on those around us. I am not saying that it's just a childhood story and we should forget about it now that we are adult. But it's a childhood story that you can step back from, look at dispassionately and say: 'Oh, what a Story that was, but I am no longer that child.'

The enduring impact of some childhood stories, however, can be so strikingly felt, and yet, the essence of these Stories themselves can be extremely hard to detect, connect with and decipher. As described earlier, some Stories are pre-memory and others we bury deeply. Much of this happens sub-consciously, or at the borderline of intent and the unintentional. Why do we do this, or why is our brain doing it for us? Sometimes it's for protection. Sometimes it's because the Stories themselves are so distressing that the fear of taking even a fleeting glance at them seems absolute and becomes overwhelming.

> I have recently experienced a senior leader who on the one hand was able to say, 'I know there must be a childhood story which drives my behaviours' and in the same breath name how they were filled with trepidation. 'I'm not sure what I might unleash? Is it normal to be nervous about doing this?' They entered a state of what David Kantor calls 'unknowing' because the stakes are high. Once shared, the possibility of this diminishes dramatically.
>
> **Jack, Coach**

It is tender, vulnerable territory on which we tread when daring to risk a deeper look at childhood story. Part of the reason for this lies in the fact that we are entering what David Kantor describes as the utter beatific innocence of a child's heart. We know it when we see it in a film, when we read it in a novel, and when we encounter it in life; we instinctively know it when a child gets hurt, when a child's heart is one big feeling of deep hurt, because it is so very evocative that it reaches straight down into our own hearts. David Kantor called it 'beatific innocence' because of the responsibility the child takes upon themselves for the very parent or adult who is hurting them. How is it possible not to love the innocent self-sacrificing child, not to want to make their pain and hurt go away?

## When the child takes responsibility and blames themselves

Children have a peculiar tendency to attribute blame to themselves. They do this even for events they simply cannot possibly be responsible for, including acts of violence by others. Children exist in a world in which they are surrounded by people who are more powerful than they are, and their ability to evade or respond is severely limited. The child can unfortunately also easily get confused about who is actually responsible, and they can end up taking the side of the aggressor and the oppressor. They identify with them. It's a painful way of reconciling the damage that has been done to them. The child accepts the dreadful Story to get an emulated experience of the love they so very clearly did not get in that Story, including convincing themselves that: "I am responsible for what happened to me". If they could not prevent the damage, they might at least be able to benefit somehow by embracing it afterwards. It is a very clever, but slippery and intricate psychological mechanism, and once it has implanted itself in the child's identity, it all too easily makes its way right into adult-identity. How to give that up? How to give up the very coping mechanism that keeps up the illusion of having at least something – maybe not real love, but something? That is the hard work to be done during Story-work. So as adults working on our Stories, we need to start with fathoming out what in our childhood we were responsible for and what we were not.

It's important for the Story-guide to be able to draw on a basic knowledge of child development in the context of working with an adult on their childhood story. For example, following Piaget, the Clinical Psychologist renowned for his pioneering work in Child Development, we know that at particular stages in children's development they will naturally try to construct very egocentric meaning out of what is happening to them. Children will put themselves at the centre and believe that they are at fault; that they are the cause for whatever happens around them; that they are responsible in a way for even the most savage abuse. For the children, there is no other explanation – they must have deserved the beatings. Why else would they have happened? Objectively, what is happening to them makes no sense, is possibly abusive, and may even be a criminal offence. Yet in their search for meaning, this attribution to Self keeps coming back. The child attributes blame to themselves, in other words, the – at that developmental stage – natural egocentricity of the child leads them to believe that it has to be something they have done or have not done, that is resulting in the parental or adult behaviour, however abhorrent such behaviour may be.

By re-engaging with these experiences of the past and relating them to current realities it becomes possible to do something about the child – or child identity, if you like – that is distorted and outdated, but lives on in the adult unmodified nevertheless. At this point, adaptive transformation needs to take place, so that the adult is no longer 'acting through the child'. Those dark things that happened to the child, happened long ago. They do not go away, but put into the right perspective, not only can their debilitating effects be warded off, they can even have a positive impact in adult life. The dark side can fuel the light. Nobody can take back the past suffering of the child. Nobody can take back the damage of a distorted internal narrative [stemming from the suffering] inflicted on the growing child and later the adult. But strength and courage are often present most vividly in the misguided and frequently desperate efforts of adults acting out their childhood stories. It is up to us to break the hold of the Story and harness that existing strength and courage for a new and brighter future. Done right, Story-work does not put you back at square one, with a clean slate, and with no strength or talents. Instead, successful Story-work helps you keep hold of the good parts, while getting rid of the toxic rubbish they got entangled with, transforming dark and dangerous energies into forces of light.

## A dilemma in daring to look

There is an ever-present dilemma:

- Continue carrying the burden of long-buried childhood stories and live with their strangely consoling familiarity, even though they are accompanied by an onerous toll on the Self and those we live and work with, or

- Take the risk to disturb a carefully – albeit subconsciously – crafted equilibrium by going to work on oneself, and take a look at these critically important Stories of the past, despite the perturbance that might come with doing so.

When we start to look at and talk about our childhood story, we free up the energy used for keeping the Story suppressed and hidden. As we unshackle ourselves from a ritualised past, our latent strength can start to rise to the surface and shine. We can feel a sense of being liberated and invigorated.

In my coaching practice, I frequently encounter people who describe their experience of daring to look at and work with their childhood story as akin to a veil being lifted. It is as if for the first time, light has shone on something that previously seemed too petrifying to explore, that was too dark to talk about or even to reveal its existence, for fear of what might occur. Most often this is a completely irrational fear, and yet, the experience is no less real, no less striking and no less blocking, just because of this objective irrationality. In light of such debilitating fear, it seems absolutely unreasonable to go there. Why would a person even dare to look in the direction of Story? The seeds of the answer can be found in the motive of the question, which talks about 'debilitating' fear. It is the hope of liberation from this fear, the hope of breaking the hold our childhood story has over us, the hope for the invigoration that comes with this newfound freedom that lie at the heart of daring to do the seemingly counter-intuitive.

> I would say to any leader that, whether you recognise it or not, your childhood story is playing a role in your leadership model and, at present, unless you are working on it, then it is having an impact that you are possibly not seeing. It may be in your blind spot and it may be having an impact in ways that you can't understand, or maybe have difficulty understanding. I would say without hesitation, that being in relationship with somebody who can work with you on your childhood story, in a way that enables you to be able to be in control of it, means that your ability to be the most effective leader that you can possibly be is now within your grasp.
>
> **Samantha, Leader**

> I think that the most valuable thing you can get from going into your childhood story is you find your

*adult voice. You find a way to be in the present and acknowledge the past, but not have it drag you back all the time. It's very healthy for both your relationships with people that you're trying to work with, but also for how you present to people. I think as a leader how you present is incredibly important. If you're going to lead, my view is you need to present to people so that they feel safe; they feel trusted, and they feel they can do their very best and it will be acknowledged. That is a huge part of your role as a leader. If you are carrying a lot of old wounds, it's hard to do that because you'll react and respond in a way that won't necessarily be constructive for the other person.*

**Ann, Director**

## Behavioural preference and comfort with daring to look

It is important not to over-generalise from behavioural reactions to the experience of engaging in Story-work. However, there are some broad propositions that can go quite a way towards explaining the range of responses a Story-guide might encounter. Below I have taken three profile examples from the nine possible permutations that exist in the Structural Dynamics model, if we put aside the Action Modes [three Operating Systems x three Communication Domains = nine]. These examples can help us understand how behavioural preferences may impact on the particular way somebody engages with their own childhood story:

### Closed Power

In this case the person may have a tendency to avoid the childhood story and/or the darker parts of it. This simply comes from not seeing the direct practical need for, and impact from, exploring this territory [which is an important factor for 'Closed Power']. People who gravitate to Closed Power most strongly may also appear not to feel much in the face of meeting others with high Affect. However, it would be wrong to assume that the need for Affect is not there, because we know from experience that it is. Important here is the particular route taken for accessing feelings and meaning, which is via Power. Any high stakes reactions will be more around saying, 'Enough, I'm out of here and if you try to stop me, I will fight you.' It is about not wanting to go there in the first place and not seeing the relevance of doing so. We know the importance of creating order, simplicity and clarity for Closed Power, so in many ways it makes sense that the person would not see the need for dropping deeply into the seeming mess and confusion that can so often lie at the heart of childhood story work. Although the need to do that very work is, of course, frequently there. There might also be a high degree of discomfort in showing emotion – and they naturally anticipate such emotional content, if they were to start exploring Story-work in depth.

## Open Affect

A person high in Open Affect may work almost too hard in getting into the dark parts of their Story and may struggle to get out of these shadowy realms. The person may also have a tendency to 'fall apart' very easily and then worry terribly having done so. Often the falling apart is for good reason in service of Self and also others, because people strong in Open Affect frequently feel things in a way others do not. As a result, they often carry the feeling for others in a team or group, and you may find them wanting to do so for you as the Story-guide too. The constant attention to, and drive towards, Affect can be a heavy burden for a person to hold when doing deep Story-work, and they may easily become exhausted. This is, in part, because being high in Open Affect essentially means allowing the Self to be vulnerable.

## Random Meaning

With a profile that is very strong in Random Meaning, the person may not have a need for others to really know them or get close to them in Affect. The preference is to be met in Meaning. In all likelihood, they may have a tendency towards lower expressions of Affect and rely on accessing feeling through their Meaning. Therefore, although appearing on the surface to others to have little Affect, this is not so. In contrast to Open Affect where the person may floridly express their feelings, someone strong in Random Meaning uses their mind and logical thought as the primary means of exploring, analysing and interpreting the childhood story. You may also find such a person wanting to move deep into explanations and context for what emerges through intense Story-work.

## Love and the childhood story

The experience of love is critical as you guide the person to look at their childhood stories, yet the concept of 'Love' in a leadership context is not common for most leaders. Despite great leaders including Martin Luther King, talking openly about love in the context of power, and global change leaders like Kahane [2010] locating love and power at the core of his theory of social change, it is highly likely that many leaders will be unaccustomed – and maybe uncomfortable – with talking about love in their professional environment. Yet, love is fundamental in the context of childhood story work, and David Kantor [2012] poses four questions about love that are central in providing a focus for any in-depth Story-work:

- Was I loved?

- Am I loved and lovable?

- Do I know how to love?

- Do I know how to be loved?

The last question potentially sums up all the rest. Do I know how to take love in? Do I let it feel good? Do I integrate it into my Self, which makes me feel worthy of being loved now, when I wasn't back then? If you don't know how to be loved, it is that much harder to overcome having not been loved in the earliest stages of life. Not knowing how to be loved can leave a hole that fills up with deep sadness.

## Need and neediness

The issues of need and neediness may well come up in your work with the Story-sharer, particularly at critical junctures where the person might be ready to drop more deeply into their Story. In need, the person is clear that they are deserving what they crave, whereas in neediness they are not sure. There is often a natural slip over from need into neediness, because of [self-] doubt about whether they are lovable at all. Maybe they once were, but for sure now as adults with all the haunting imprints of the childhood story that reside within, they are convinced that they cannot possibly be so. Unfortunately, it is but a small step from feeling unlovable to not knowing how to be loved. In those moments when a person regresses into neediness, it is seldom an appealing sight, and can be a 'turn-off' for those around them. People's neediness is repelling the very love and understanding they seek, and consequently ensuring a self-fulfilling prophecy of not getting the love they yearn for. There may even be an accompanying tendency to push away the love they do receive. This can happen even though this love is coming from a person they desperately want to love them. If present, this is a critical, acutely problematic and painful issue that needs to be attended to when working towards writing the new internal narrative [See Chapter 9].

Equally important is to be aware of the notion that a Story-guide who goes deep could inadvertently reinforce a Story-sharer's neediness by somehow holding the person in their Story too long or by creating a dependency in the relationship. Conversely, the depth of the need displayed by some Story-sharers may put some Story-guides off; they may not feel comfortable to do Story-work of such intensity. This is one reason why, for Story-guides, knowing their own Self broadly and deeply with all its assorted preferences and aversions, and having a clear Practice Model for doing this work, is so imperative. We can hear this in Rebecca's reflection below:

> As I think about my own experience of working on my Story, it would have done irreparable damage if I had begun to go to these depths and then found that the Story-guide was not up for it. It would have reinforced the shame and anxiety about having shared what I did. I think it is vital that a Story-guide really understands the depths that this work could take them to before they begin.
>
> **Rebecca, Coach**

## Expressions of anger

Anger is often significant when working in the depths of Story. Anger can be turned inwards in the form of sadness, a lack of self-worth, a belief that the person is not lovable or not worthy to receive love. The self-censoring can go so far as to assert that they do not have the right to be angry at what happened to them in their childhood story. In so doing, they are confirming the primal impression that the child took from whatever happened to them, for example, worthlessness, un-lovability. It is a clever psychological trick, because it keeps the person from ever truly moving forwards, which in this case would mean genuinely accepting that they have every right to be loved.

Anger doesn't always have to be negative. It can be healthy and life-affirming when it gives somebody the strength to break out of old bonds and dysfunctional beliefs. It can be an expression of strong determination to overcome something. Anger and determination can often be manifestations of the same thing expressed differently. Both co-exist on the path towards the writing of the new internal narrative. Anger can be expressed in all manner of ways, including through the act of overcoming the debilitating effects of the childhood story.

## Perceived threat

The perception of threat can act as a block for a leader as they contemplate embarking on Story-work, especially where the Story takes them into areas that are private, stressful or intimate. They may also fear the threat of sanction. This relates specifically to contexts where the possibility exists that information revealed through working on their Story could stigmatise or incriminate them in some way. Similarly, if Story-work impinges on political alignments, or a carefully cultivated public persona, it may be perceived as problematic. Defining 'political' in its broadest sense, there is real potential for Story-work to be seen as threatening, particularly by people in positions of power within an organisation. John really captures the dilemma this presents to leaders in what he says here:

> *I've spent 30 years cultivating a narrative about my leadership, and me, which, in part, is why the Board appointed me in the midst of this crisis. If they or the organisation find out I'm working on my childhood story, I'll lose all credibility and respect and yet it's exactly what I need to do to be the leader this place needs right now!*
> **John, CEO**

## Core components of Story-work

There are a number of core components that you can draw on as you begin to work with an individual leader on their Story which are listed below:

- A good environment is important; make sure you have privacy, a comfortable space, no external disturbances and sufficient time.

- Encourage the person to rest, to develop a relaxation routine, to eat well and healthily, in general to take care of body and soul. These factors are essential for creating the container in which Story-work can take place.

- Prepare well and create an agenda. Ask the Story-sharer to do the same i.e. to create their own agenda for how they want to use the time dedicated to exploring their childhood story so that they get what they need from the sessions.

- Let the Story-sharer take the lead in setting the agenda for the early sessions and encourage them to help you design the frame for the time you spend working together.

- Point out that there are light and dark zones for exploration and draw attention to both the light and dark characteristics arising out of the childhood story.

- Play back the actual words the Story-sharer is using and follow the person around in the places they take you and you take them to in their childhood story.

- Look for the strange nuances of the internal narrative.

- Validate the stubborn persistence of any shadows.

- Search out the key to why the internal narrative got laid down.

- Be skilful in the use of silence; make conscious and deliberate choices about when and how you use silence in this work.

- Work in the feeling zone using a two-fold approach – i.e. seek out opportunities to get to the feelings underneath the childhood story and the childhood story underneath the feelings.

- Name any attributions [regarding something as being caused by another person or a thing] you are making about aspects of the childhood story, what you are hearing and the picture you are forming as you analyse what is being revealed for the Story-sharer to push and pull on.

- When, from all your preparation and planning for sessions you think you know where things are with the person you are working with, remember to check this out. You may be off track even when you don't think that that's the case.

- When the person is finding it hard to switch out of their old internal narrative you can task them in the following way: "Talk yourself out of the hour. What do you need to say? Take as much time as you need. How old are you feeling at this moment having told me all that you did? What's important about that age?"

- Make predictions about what is possible or what could be possible for the person in terms of a new internal narrative as a form of conscious intervention. Note the nature and level of reactivity to you doing so and go to work on that reactivity.

- Be disciplined in keeping notes of every session.

## Revisiting the past

As the work in daring to look progresses, you may find that the Story-sharer wants to deflect or minimise the childhood story to make it smaller, and not really relevant. In so doing, they may in some way be underestimating the impact of the Story as they revisit the past. For others, they may over-exaggerate or over-tell it. This doesn't really matter. It's not the point. The daring to look and the explicit telling of the childhood story is what is important.

> For a very long time, I felt like there was no point in telling my Story because nothing was ever going to change what had happened to me, but I was still having nightmares from time to time and my Story was getting triggered too. That was the point. Michael asked me to connect with the child and to really tell her Story.
>
> **Sarah, Author**

There is always a debate about whether to get back into the experience or to stay well away from it. In this context, you need to take a decision about whether to encourage the person to make more of the Story rather than less of it, so that they can really explore it with the ultimate goal of placing the Story in the past where it belongs. This means not forgetting what happened, but finding a way to live with it – developing the new internal narrative about what happened.

## Daring to look, then sharing the Story

In sharing the childhood story with others, it loses its power. The internal narrative about it starts losing its tight grip almost instantaneously too. However, the roughest period of the sharing of darker parts of the Story is once it has been voiced. This is because the Story is with the person again; it's there, right in front of them. It's no longer being suppressed. It's near the surface and the person may not be liking themselves because of what they are seeing and experiencing. Having not talked about something for a very long time or maybe never having looked at it before, through the telling of the Story it can become so present for the person that it may feel unbearable to them. Through sharing and making public what happened, the feelings associated with the childhood story can come rushing back. If this is the case, it is essential to stay with the person and their Story. You need to talk about it.

## Disclosure of Story at the very end of a session

There is no single way to deal with the situation whereby a person discloses a part of their childhood story so dark that it is clearly disturbing them in some way, right before the end of a session. Unfortunately, this often happens and can be because the disclosure contains content that they are uncomfortable to talk about which is why they leave it until the very end. However, they might also disclose something in this way to test out how it feels to say it, knowing that they won't have to delve into it more deeply because it is right at the end of the session.

To deal with it, you need to find a way to help them to ease out of it, such that they are not tempted to retreat again. You need to be clear with them that you are glad they have shared as freely and deeply as they have done, and that you want them to return to it at the beginning of the next session. You can also diffuse the situation by helping them to see the positive in the act of sharing itself. Treat the sharing of that part of the childhood story as a starting point and name it as such. Invite curiosity about what has been coming to the surface. Point out that you are in search of something good to come out of it; something that can be really transformative.

## The 'work to do' in daring to look

*A summary*

- Explicitly and deliberately contract and set clear boundaries for the work to allay any fears or threats that may be present.

- Build the relationship between the Story-guide and sharer into a safe container within which the work can take place.

- Bring the childhood story to the surface and name it.

- Explore the childhood story with all its complexity.

- Go ever more deeply to reach into the subterranean levels of the Story.

- Expand the Story-sharer's awareness of how the childhood story manifests in the moment through an internal narrative.

- Greet the existing internal narrative with compassion and love, even if it is jarring and dysfunctional.

- Make friends with the Self in the existing internal narrative.

- Open to the possibility and exploration of a new internal narrative that could be invigorating and life-affirming.

- Step fully into the uncertainty and confusion that frequently exists when you enter the space between the existing or old internal narrative and the newly emerging one.

- Respect, integrate and take command of the old and the new internal narratives.

- Expect retrenchment, work with it and at the same time do all that is possible to fully embrace and embody the new internal narrative.

# Chapter 5

## Go Deep

### Befriending the complex challenges in childhood story-work

*"Whenever we enter our past and encounter strong feelings, we are close to the centre of our being. Typically, we are frightened off from the healing waters, which await us there and don't penetrate deeply enough into the Story."*

### David Kantor

### Fear gets in the way of going deeper

Fear presents us with a complex challenge to overcome because of how it blocks and keeps us trapped in our childhood stories. At a poetry festival in the UK back in 1994, I heard Maya Angelou say:

*"There is no greater burden than a story untold."*

Overcoming the fear to reveal and tell your childhood story requires such visceral power that it really is an expression of ultimate courageousness. Even for those who might describe their childhood stories as 'trivial', fear can still surface, and there can be accompanying shame in the simple act of voicing out loud that imperfect love existed for them.

What can help to ease this fear of Story? Really encouraging the person to push their behavioural repertoire with you, their Story-guide, plays a critical role. The Story-guide creates a testing ground for the person to go more deeply into their childhood story. The focus is on supporting the Story-sharer to challenge profoundly held beliefs within their internal narrative as they begin to model new and different ways of being with quicker reaction times.

I can share an example of this from the very earliest Story-work sessions I did with Michael during which he named the importance of me being able to Oppose him. He had detected early on the significant challenge this would present in my being able to do so because of how low Oppose was in my repertoire. This, in turn, signposted him to the notion that there must be a Story sitting back of such a low propensity for offering correction. But before going directly there, he also named how detrimental an inability to Oppose on my part could be in our coaching relationship.

Here's why; he was a stuck Mover communicating largely in the language of Meaning. One of the ways this behavioural preference showed itself was that in some of our coaching sessions he would get incredibly carried away in providing me with lots of different examples for how and why I might approach something in a particular way – and I would let him. This was, in part, because he did a good job and was such a good teacher, and, in part, because I wanted to learn from him. However, it was also because of my difficulty in offering an Oppose, especially in a relationship of this kind that was so important to me. My experiences meant that fear would block me from Opposing him, even when I knew that's precisely what I should have done.

His naming of the importance of me being able to Oppose him, led me to recognise that I needed to develop my antennae for sizing up any dangers in the coaching environment with him – in different ways with more discrimination and criticism rather than fear. Fear would have led me to be compliant rather than to be putting a different voice out there i.e. one that said, 'Wait a minute, I will not be dominated; I do have a voice of my own. I will speak out – I may shout out – hey, I've got better ideas than you.' In naming this at the beginning of our work together, it became possible to test and play with the structure he was getting at early on, but also to be serious about it.

**Sarah, Author**

This is a great illustration of how you can use the coaching context to explicitly name the change that is needed, and begin to offer some ideas for ways of achieving that change.

> As we went deeper into the Story, we also drew out the link to anger in all its variations such as scepticism, frustration and irritation as well as anger itself. I had experienced rage from my parents as a child, this was part of my Story. As a result, I was hugely fearful of anger; I suppressed it in myself and avoided it in others. I needed to explore what this did to the freedom I had professionally and personally to express anger and the implications of that. Because of my experience I did not allow myself to express legitimate anger and, having surfaced this and identified what I needed to do, I now needed to practice.
>
> I recall how Michael set himself up as a figure I could practice on – literally! He invited me to be angry with him when I needed to, in fact he said that he looked forward to those moments or opportunities and expressed his hope that I would feel the freedom to strike back appropriately when things happened in our work together.
>
> **Sarah, Author**

This is an example of the importance of enabling the person you are working with to make connections between aspects of their behavioural repertoire and different components of their childhood story, as well as coming to know what the connections are about. In this case, the dangers associated with Opposing in my childhood story contributed to my weak Oppose. Therefore, a primary focus for me was to expand my behavioural repertoire by strengthening and integrating the Oppose into my interactions without aversion or fear. It gave me significantly more power to act and put me in a position to begin to explore the question:

> "How am I limited by this manifestation of my childhood story and my internal narrative about it?' or 'How am I allowing this part of my childhood story and internal narrative to limit my behavioural choices and range?"

## The place of shame in Story-work

Fear can also make itself known through explicit or implicit questioning of the Story-guide:

- Are you going to abandon me?

- Are you going to go away if I tell you these horrible things about myself; if I tell you these horrible things that happened to me?

There is an important link to shame here too.

Shame is with the Story-sharer, and with the Story-sharer only. For the Story-guide, there is no shame no matter what is shared. The Story-sharer will, of course, doubt this. It takes time to trust. It takes time to build the container in the relationship. We all have another life, a personal and professional life in which we want to please and be regarded highly. By sharing the darker parts of the childhood story with the Story-guide, embarrassment and shame can arise.

The Story-sharer's fear can be that our regard for them will in some way be contaminated by details which may be humiliating for them. When we as Story-guides engage in Story-work with people we are asking them to trust that in sharing their experiences with us, all will be well. Be assured that every detail from the dark side of peoples' lives will be of crucial importance to them. And we must preserve and protect peoples' dignity when they share things with us this closely.

Only if the Story-sharer feels safe, will they really talk in depth about their Story, and talking about the details of what happened in the childhood story can be so important if we really are to help people make their 'way through' past suffering and transform the internal narrative that emanates from it. Below Rebecca shares her experience of this when she was working with me as her Story-guide:

> It was a huge step for me to start to talk about my childhood story. I had spent my life working in rigid, formal environments where there was no space for such reflection and an active resistance to even the suggestion of this type of work. I was also part of other systems, which would have said this was soft, fluffy and irrelevant – ancient history.

*So with a deep breath, I started to share a Story that I had never spoken about – not with my colleagues or friends or even my family. I can't tell you how acutely I scrutinised Sarah's response. I was looking for the slightest sign of judgement. That was what I expected and it would have confirmed that this really was a ludicrous idea to start talking about these Stories all these years later. It would also have validated my belief that I didn't deserve to have my Story heard – it was not important – and I had no right to feel any kind of emotion about it.*

*There was definitely no judgement – not even a flicker. But nor was there collusion. There was no move to assuage, nor any kind of condemnation of anyone implicated in the Story – there was just a firm, kind reassurance that this was OK. That it was valid and reasonable. More than that, it was transformative.*

*As I left that session, Sarah said to me, 'You know, that Story can never be the same again. Now you've shared it, it will have changed in nature.' I honestly didn't know what she meant.*

*I do now. Over time, the potency of that Story has gone. It is just a Story – some words on a page, or the narration of a sequence of events. It's not a reality that I live and breathe each day. It has lost its power over me.*

**Rebecca, Coach**

The Story-guide's response to somebody's Story is only borne out of really wanting to know the Story-sharer deeply. This stems from the belief that deeply knowing another human being is the most profound connection possible, and is also what love is all about. So knowing the darkest parts of someone you care about only increases the depth of the connection and the depth of the love you feel. This is so simple for the person hearing the childhood story – not so easy on the part of the Story-sharer. As a result, it is very important that this message about 'strengthening connection' is conveyed well. In other words, let the Story-sharer know that you comprehend and appreciate them so much better for them having shared these parts of their childhood story with you. Know that it can be hard for them to really embrace this for themselves, because of the shame involved, and because you are talking about the delicate topic of love here, for which we have almost not left any respectable place in Western Society outside a limited romantic notion.

When receiving information from the Story-sharer, particularly of a more sensitive nature, or where shame is present, there is a sense in which the Story-guide is simply bearing witness to their experience and is coming to know them more deeply. So the response might be akin to conveying something as simple as – 'Oh, so this is more of Sarah Hill that I am coming to know.' Somehow such straightforward confirmation of witnessing adds value to the thoughts and feelings for the person sharing. In turn, the loyalty and trust between the Story-sharer and Story-guide keeps growing and strengthening the more the person shares of their Story.

There can also be a natural anxiety that accompanies the sharing of the childhood story, so we need to find ways to support the person to ease up on that. It happens, it is what it is, but we want to see the anxiety disappear over time. The Story-guide becomes someone who simply knows the person's Story and appreciates them even more for knowing it, because that is how it is. If the anxiety persists, a good and simple question to pose could be: "What would the anxiety be about at this point?"

> Shame was a constant presence and manifested in so many different ways for me. How it showed up right away was in the realisation that for a long time I had carried a deeply entrenched and buried fear that if others knew the whole Story; if they knew it all and if I really revealed the depths and darkest parts of my childhood experience that I would not be respected and that I would not be loved. That was the construct.
>
> In helping me to reveal these dark Stories Michael kept inviting me to trust him. He expressed his care for me and I found myself psychologically entertaining the possibility that, yes, I might really be able to trust him and that maybe, just maybe, I could let myself be loved and cared for by him. Yet it was so hard to do. For a long time, the depth of the shame I felt blocked my being

*able to really talk about the darker parts of the Story. The mental model I had was that I had let things happen to me as a child; that I hadn't found a way to stop the abuse happening; that I had in some way allowed it to happen. His response when I named the shame in this way was: 'Hmm, what a phenomenon!' He went on to remind me of what he had told me in earlier sessions about how the child psychologically finds a way to take responsibility for what happens to her. He was so accurate. I felt that what happened was my fault; that I was to blame. My own sense about that time was that I had had the power that I had now as an adult, which, of course, the child simply does not and never can have. Nevertheless, at that time the child felt like an adult and in the here and now the adult couldn't remember ever feeling like a child. The child was supposed to have been taken care of. She wasn't supposed to be fending off abuse.*

*In daring to look and explore the experience of shame, what we were trying to do was to put my history in perspective in such a way that it would allow me to fully enjoy the fruits of my capacities. Painful as it was, it was necessary. What I did in slowly trusting Michael over time, and telling him my Story, was that I began opening the possibility for a new internal narrative to emerge; one in which I was good and loving and lovable. The sharing of the Story initially left me feeling fearful and concerned about having done so – he named that this was completely understandable and then went on to play back to me the experience of being on the receiving end. He said that the more he got to know me the more he loved me. It seemed paradoxical to me – and it was – but there was no judgement in him about my Story and no judgement in the knowing of it. He said he felt connected to the child and to the adult. I cried tears of relief in the connection and in beginning to unburden myself of the Story I had been carrying for such a long time. He stressed how much he wanted me to understand that there was only deep appreciation for the person he was getting to know – me.*

**Sarah, Author**

## Coherence and confusion

Inherent within the process of Story-work and the writing of the new internal narrative are cycles of confusion, trying to make sense of things and getting lost before coming clearer and gaining new insights. One way for the Story-guide to interpret and shed light on the confusion is that it is a mess of Affect [feelings] and Meaning [thoughts] that are all intertwined and need untangling. There often comes a time during the process whereby, as an adult, the Story-sharer can understand the childhood story and all that goes with that, but through the eyes of the child who lives on within, it is still confusing, deeply confusing. The adult may feel known and loved, but the child may continue to feel wounded and scared for a long time. Helping the 'child within' to recover represents the next phase of the work to be done. Can the child within draw strength, comfort and love from the adult? We have to strengthen the adult aspects in the 'inner child' of the adult. As the Story-guide, we need to know when it is the child that is speaking or reacting to us, and when it is the adult. We also need to know when it is the voice of Affect and when it is Meaning or Power that is being expressed. We need to be able to discern these different voices. Different choices open up as a result of being able to do so [see Chapter 10 for more about this].

> *Michael always opened up and tied together a lot of things with me. To him there was coherence in what was emerging even from the earliest sessions. To me I was swimming around in abject confusion a lot of the time. The fact that he was seeing the picture helped me so much. He also tried to play back some of that coherence to me, but was clear that he did not expect me to get the whole thing. As we went deeper into the Story we built parts of the map, which became visual and readable to him and, in time, to me too.*

> *An example: I constantly expressed my doubts about my worth in doing the work with Michael and I also constantly searched for data to reinforce the doubts. However, from the outset Michael saw me as worthy, as very worthy, and this challenged everything I believed or felt about myself. This was the total opposite of everything I had experienced with my parents. He saw me as really good and he sewed himself into my Story to help me resolve*

*the demons left over from my past and to write a new internal narrative about the Story. Somehow, I had preserved a lot of well-being and health even in the midst of horrendous psychological and physical abuse. He not only saw my core strength, but he also connected me to what was at the root of my belief that I was unworthy. I felt bad that I had that core strength and that I had survived so well and intact when other members of my family had not. I felt guilty. To the extent that I kept succeeding, I distanced myself more and more from my family, and from my childhood experiences. I was on top of the world I was creating and building and it felt magnificent. Michael's challenge to me was to accept my success. I had absolutely no clue what on earth he was talking about. His challenge left me utterly confused. Back then.*

**Sarah, Author**

As you begin to introduce new kinds of truths – such as the one in my own Story-work about being worthy – into the interpretation of the childhood story and its effects, know that further confusion may emerge. You may confuse the Story-sharer as you begin to break through and see connections. However, be alert to the fact that one way to interpret the confusion, especially if it is repeated, is that it may simply be another device to throw you off track, because you ask the Story-sharer to stand on new ground. Confusion requires you to be smart and thorough, because in dealing with confusion in the Story-sharer, you – as the Story-guide – have to work even harder to help the person traverse it. It can seem as though the Story-sharer is confused cognitively, but know that the confusion may actually emanate emotionally. The reason they don't understand cognitively is because they do not understand emotionally. In other words, there is a tangled mess of emotions such as sadness, disappointment and joy that are all entwined and leading to the confusion. Such confusion may also be a form of challenge-cum-invitation to you from the Story-sharer. They are saying to you 'help me through the confusion, help me to understand.' You are asking them to stand on new ground and that can be so very challenging and indeed confusing.

*I am thinking about those moments when your Story-guide has spotted something and named that thing, which on naming is so completely obvious and yet, so completely not obvious to you. Albeit that it can bring with it a lot of confusion to begin with, certainly, the Story-guide pointing to something that was absolutely in my blindfold was incredibly powerful and I think it wasn't just a naming of it. It was helping me to think about what to do with it, because recognising that something exists is one thing, putting it in the context of what your current experiences are is another and I think that's a huge skill. For me it was just so revelatory.*

**Samantha, Leader**

## The place of writing in exploring and resolving confusion

Writing can quickly become a refuge and saviour particularly during times when the confusion, chaos and complexity of the childhood story becomes too much. Writing is a way to Bystand the Self, to reflect on feelings, thoughts and actions in Meaning. We know that Bystanding in Meaning is the most effective way of lowering the stakes for Self and others, and it always provided that for me. There were many times when I became so lost in the childhood story that I needed reminding of this.

Writing also helps in being able to place events in the childhood story in the timeline where they belong. The timing of events in the childhood story can easily become confused. It is almost as though experiences from the past are taking place in the current time. It certainly can feel that way when a trigger results in a high stakes reaction. Have you ever felt like you have been transported back in time to being a child of a certain age and feeling as though you are standing in front of your head teacher or parent or authority figure of some kind? It can be hard to locate the adult Self in the present moment when this is happening. This means we need to help the Story-sharer to place events in the time in which they took place. By working through the events consciously and sorting, naming and labelling them, by making the past explicit, we increase the possibilities that the past will lose its implicit grip on us. As a result, it becomes less likely that we will be catapulted back into emotional turmoil now as adults, even if high stakes triggers are present.

*My experience was akin to sorting out a filing cabinet, placing everything in the order in which it had*

*occurred, honouring what had gone before and really
acknowledging and befriending each experience before
placing it in the bigger order of things. In my own case,
there were gaping holes with files missing that needed
to be retrieved, there were papers within files that had
become unreadable and there were files that were stuck
so far back in the depths of the cabinet that I did not even
know they were there.*

**Sarah, Author**

## Writing as a support-vehicle

Writing can provide a support-vehicle for going more deeply into the darkest zones of the childhood story where shame and embarrassment reside.

*I wrote story after story for Michael as a way of revealing
certain aspects of my experiences of abuse and whilst I
found it extremely hard to do, it was not so hard as to say
it out loud without having written it first. The writing also
left me feeling freer to talk about the extent and detail of
the abuse, having written it first and shared that writing
with Michael.*

**Sarah, Author**

Michael then posed the question: 'What is your sense of my hearing or reading darker narratives of this kind? Are you worried about it?'

*My answer to this question was 'yes and no' – I was a
bit worried about it, but I was also putting my trust
in him by sharing it with him and I was doing so with a
clear purpose of gaining command of the childhood
story, transforming and writing the new internal
narrative.*

**Sarah, Author**

Writing in the third person can be enormously helpful. I wrote about the child, Sarah. These quasi-fictional and amplified accounts all helped with entering the darker parts of the experience:

*In the small hours of the morning before the sun began
to rise, she lay in her bed wakeful and heavy with the*

*tumultuous, random wanderings of her confused mind. The black and white tiles of the kitchen floor familiar from so long ago were drifting back and forth in her consciousness; that cringing feeling in her body as she shrank back into that private place of safety that much later became her brilliant mind. She recalled the cold smoothness of the linoleum as she regained consciousness after a particularly vicious beating. Yet for now, in this moment, she continued to wander and each time she went a little bit further, a little bit deeper in to the recesses of that dark time, that dark place where she had felt so alone.*

**Writing sample from Sarah, Author**

## Translating dreams and disturbing memories through writing

When working on childhood story, intrusive thoughts and memories can sometimes emerge so rapidly that they flood the person and threaten to overwhelm them. The history represented by the childhood story can also really crowd in at night during sleep, and the kind of dreams a person has are often a reflection of that. It is possible to make up a hypothesis about what the dreams are evoking in order to explore this with the person.

*My experience in sleep was one in which I would lie down in the foetal position, hands tucked in, protecting myself from being grabbed while sleeping, which had actually happened to me a few times when I was very young. I felt endangered and I needed to protect myself. This was completely antithetical to what a childhood experience should have been like. I suddenly caught sight of the fact that even as an adult I would fold myself up so that I was inaccessible. At a very deep level, I came to realise that I was settling down to go to sleep with a deep-rooted fear that I would be woken and hit. I would go to sleep afraid and guarded. I was ready for something terrible to happen. My childhood story was showing up even there.*

**Sarah, Author**

This kind of interference into other public/private living is common when going deeper into the shadows of the childhood story, so it is important to provide a process or activity that enables the person to take command of their thoughts. One way to do this is to have them write the thoughts out as they are forming – day or night – in real time journaling. So no editing, just writing each thought as it surfaces and to keep writing until the waves of thought eventually begin to recede. The person may kick back, unable to see how such a simple activity could possibly help them. But it is hard to look up from troubled waters when you are lost in the turbulence and storm of negative thoughts. You can also ask the person to write an account with a theme that is pertinent to them – in my case – this would have been a description of how to overcome cruelty from the child's perspective.

In doing this writing, it can be helpful to guide the person to create some quasi-fictional characters or fairy tales, and then use the thoughts that are arising in a written piece. There are many writers who do exactly this themselves. Frequently this is what much of the best fiction is made of. Authors take their nightmare thoughts and experiences to create interesting characters, because their demons are truly 'fantastic'. This is another extension of the process of 'taking command'. If the Story-sharer can take this step of transforming troubling thoughts into characters of fantastical form or even horror stories, progress becomes possible. The burden of the person's history no longer needs to be carried inside them, upsetting their sleep, disrupting their days, undermining their sense of themselves. Instead it is converted into a creative exercise. So have them write the thoughts as fiction, using characters that take reality to the extreme. Urge them not to embellish with pure fantasy, but to write it like the script for a movie they already saw in their head.

Writing out an account in this way can also trigger a shame response in the person, so be ready to go to work on that if needed.

> *I remember the first time I did what I am suggesting here, having woken in the night and found myself unable to return to sleeping, because of the thoughts that were rampaging through my mind. When I woke in the morning, I tore the notepad into the tiniest of pieces afraid that anyone else might read what was written. In the sessions with Michael, I shared what was there. I remembered the black and white tiles on the kitchen floor after the beating from my parents. The physical sensation of humiliation at*

*having been beaten was palpable. It was almost like an*
*aura. It was as though I was feeling the humiliation all over*
*again. I was talking about the feeling of powerlessness*
*and describing this feeling in words and images and it*
*was hard to do. However, what was wonderful was that*
*writing the thoughts as a story had given me a powerful*
*means of expression. I could separate off the effects of*
*those horrific experiences into creating a written account*
*and this proved to be the trick for getting out from*
*being under such an aura.*

**Sarah, Author**

It can be extremely beneficial for the Story-sharer, if the Story-guide can suggest a range of writing activities such as the ones described here because of how they support the process of putting the childhood story into its rightful place in time. It is not an easy task to succeed in, but the goal of enabling them to take command of the Story and its impact, makes it more than worth the effort.

# Chapter 6

## Face The Crises

### Traversing the pitfalls, twists and turns of deep Story-work

*"Deep into that darkness peering, I stood there, wondering, fearing, doubting, dreaming dreams no mortal ever dared to dream before."*

**Edgar Allan Poe**

### Crisis can occur after revelation of shadow experiences

Feelings of not liking the Self can often arise in the Story-sharer after revealing dark aspects of the childhood story. It is therefore extremely important to provide reassurance to the Story-sharer by expressing your truest feelings about them. This is critical, given that they have shared their innermost and unspoken experiences with you. It is both an honour and a privilege to bear witness to someone else's Story, and my own experience as a Story-guide has confirmed that consistently.

> I needed a lot of reassurance from Michael during the darkest parts of the exploration. He was consistent and persistent in how he reassured me. He expressed his concern and warm caring and that he had no judgement about what he was hearing at all apart from his sadness about the terrible cruelty that exists in the world. That I had been subject to awful experiences led to him knowing me more and therefore appreciating and ultimately loving me more. I was carrying internalised negative feelings. The negativity was in me. It was not in him. He kept telling me he was with me in the struggle; that I was not alone.
>
> **Sarah, Author**

There is also a risk that the Story-sharer might feel re-traumatised by revisiting the childhood story. Our job as practitioners is to help the person to put the old internal narrative – having emanated subconsciously from the childhood story – in a place where it no longer does harm to the adult. Check in with the Story-sharer whether they are re-experiencing [emotionally re-living] their previous experience; be alert and attentive to it as a real possibility. Often this shows itself in tangible bodily reactions, such as sweating, shortness of breath or involuntary agitation of limbs. It is always an option for you to help the person to temporarily ease back from going so deeply into the events of their childhood story. On the other hand, it might be helpful to enable and encourage them to stay right at the edge – deeply emotionally touched by their own Story – but with enough support from the Story-guide to avoid succumbing to the intensity of their past experiences. The last thing we want is for the Story-sharer to feel like they are on an emotional 'runaway train' or drowning in their sorrow.

Being alone with their Story can be terribly stressful. Working with a Story-guide, the person is no longer on their own, the Story-guide is sharing it with them. In essence, you are asking them to turn over their childhood story to you. The Story does not – and should not – hold the same meaning or feeling for you. But, the more you as the Story-guide mean to the Story-sharer, the more you can be with them and the more familiar you can become with what they are dealing with, the more of the burden you can share. I have experienced this myself many times with the people I have worked with. There arose a genuine feeling of wanting to ease their burden in me as their Story-guide.

## Withdrawal and pushing away as a form of protection

When the Story-work is underway, you may sense that the 'container' is getting stronger, but then the Story-sharer suddenly seems to withdraw. This can be read as a form of protection or self-preservation, whereby the Story-sharer is clearly indicating that they feel the need to back off for some reason. It is unfortunately only too easy for the person to get in their own way of changing. Bailing out at a critical moment of a transformative experience – even though all the help needed to achieve durable change is close at hand – is one way in which this happens. The focus should be on uncovering what is really happening in these moments when the 'urge to withdraw' surfaces, and then exploring it together. This urge to withdraw can be treated as a sign that the person is aware – at least implicitly – that there is more to come and is ready to dig deeper, if there is proper support for them to do so. In fact, the attempt to withdraw might be an implicit test for the strength and reliability of the support available for the next steps, providing a powerful rationale to 'stick with it'.

When the childhood story becomes vividly present, having really set things in motion for the Story-sharer, and beginning to go to subterranean levels, there is a definite need to give plenty of space and time. The feeling for the Story-sharer as well as the Story-guide can be that of 'being on to something' – particularly having come through significant perturbance and all the discomfort associated with that. It is important for both the Story-sharer and the guide to maintain presence and impetus in the work at this point.

It is also critically important to have confidence in the notion that any testing in the relationship between Story-guide and sharer is a welcome thing, and such testing will surely appear as the darker parts of the Story are discovered. Although it is good that memories come up to the surface and are explored, it can still be horribly painful for the person when it happens. An urge to withdraw is only too understandable then. The darkness re-visited may not let any wholesome feelings in.

Do not be scared away from the person's pain and the tangled way it might show itself. Do not back off from it or them. Exercise the choice of staying with it and them. You not only have to deal with the pain the person is experiencing, but also with their [and potentially your own] self-defeating urge to back out. These are two different things. By stepping back, they are implicitly asking you fundamental questions of the following kind:

- Will you respond to my needs?

- Are you somebody I can really trust with the darkest information about myself and will you still love and respect me?

- Will I be worthy in your eyes if I dig deeper in the sharing of my childhood story?

### Premature endings: The Story-sharer

At the height of any turbulence associated with exploring the childhood story, the feeling for the Story-sharer can be one of being frustrated, defeated or depleted, and the desire to bury aspects of the Story again, or to stop the Story-work completely, can be overwhelming.

**Story-guide:** What would stopping now do for you?

From the Story-sharer's perspective, stopping would call a halt. The perception might be that things would feel better, that they would not have to think about it anymore, that they would not have to have the more difficult shame-filled feelings.

**Story-guide:** Let's think about this together. Is the sense you have that if you were to stop, the cause and the focus on the experiences and the damage they have done would go away; that you would not think about them anymore?

It could seem to the Story-sharer that by committing to having the conversations with the Story-guide, they are forced to remember and continue to experience the pain. That way the guide's attempt to help feels instead like a bad experience that the Story-sharer instinctively wants to avoid. It is almost as if the Story-guide has joined the Story-sharer's psychological enemies by wanting to help. This is a peculiar paradox:

> *"The Story-guide stops being a source of comfort and becomes a reminder of the sources of pain."*

The paradox puts both the Story-sharer and the Story-guide in a bind:

> *"I am not sure you are right, but you are thinking that if I go away, you will feel better."*

However, it is actually like saying to the Doctor who you go to for help:

> *"I understand that the tablets you have given me are curative, but after taking them – in the short term – I don't feel so great, so I am not taking them. Don't make me."*

In these moments, the Story-guide can be perceived like an oppressor by the Story-sharer. It is as though the helper is suddenly threatening them in some way. The dread of feeling unsafe, and the resulting avoidance to continue can then become part of the problem.

Remember also that a simple but highly effective way for someone to not ask for help is to avoid the helper. It can be so very difficult for some people to request help. This can run deep. For example, a person can make the implicit assumption that asking for help would be too much or wrong in some way. You need to look out for this, because the fear of asking for help can be the real issue, rather than the overt problem that is presenting itself, which looks like inexplicably not wanting to continue.

> *My own call for help was: 'Don't help, it's too painful' alongside, 'Please don't let me convince you that it's too painful and go away.' There were so many twists and turns to my getting help and the difficulty I had in doing so. Working myself to exhaustion was one strategy I had adopted and doing so was both good and not so good. The good bit was that when I focused on other people, working very hard and creating an impossible schedule, I didn't have to think about myself, I closed down any space to do that; I didn't have to get help. It was a pretty clever way of reinforcing the child's experience of being totally alone and having no faith that anyone would want to help. The not so good bit was that it was keeping me trapped in my Story. If I was worthless, why should anyone claim that I was worthy to receive help? If I was unlovable, why should they help me and why should they want to? Even though I had been pushing Michael away, it would have been disastrous if he had done what I was asking him to do and gone away. I was approaching a threshold of change, I was right up against it and things naturally intensify when this happens.*
>
> **Sarah, Author**

The twists and turns can be astonishingly clever. The person becomes trapped in their own trap. In these situations, the conversation needs to be about the act of getting help and the paradoxical phenomenon of them finding ways not to get it.

**Story-sharer:** You can't make it better, because I won't let you!

**Story-guide:** You can even think of me as a threat to the profound belief that you are bad and by putting me in a position of impotence you think you are winning and you are not. I am not going away. I see through you and you cannot push me away. You could hang up, you could write a note saying, 'You are a failure' and I would ignore that as well. Or you could say, 'Help me love myself.'

You are in a battle in this moment. The person is going to fight you. Stay with them and with the fact that it is their internal narrative that is driving them. They may push and push and push you away. Although it may seem counter-intuitive, encourage them to be even meaner with you.

**Story-guide:** Success depends on who wins the fight, the dark self-hating part of the Self or the person you have chosen to help you win the battle. I am not going anywhere.

**Story-guide:** What would happen if you were being embraced [metaphorically] in this moment?

**Story-sharer:** I'd fight you. I'd stop you.

The person is not really fighting you off. They are fighting themselves or characters in their childhood story so as to maintain their old internal narrative. Or they really want the embrace, but cannot accept it, or perhaps cannot accept 'wanting it'. The threat of wanting something is that you might get it, or you might not.

**Story-guide:** It's not about the people in your Story. It's about you. Change is in your hands.

### Sample intervention for going even deeper

If you notice the Story-sharer's freedom to talk about things gradually increases, but you still feel there is a need to go even deeper, then an intervention of the following kind, using the metaphor of darkness and light, may be helpful:

**Story-guide:** There's a dark childhood story, you need a torch, take the torch into the dark and invite the dawn to come along. Take my hand and I will come with you into that place to explore it. Do you want to try it? Stay with this just a little while longer and tell me how far away you are from wanting to try to have a conversation with the child within?

**Story-guide:** Take my hand, wander around, use all your senses, do you hear anything? Do you feel anything?

The person may stand on the edge of the metaphorical darkness for a time, finding it hard to go there. If this happens, step in to that space yourself and wait for them to follow. Let them know that you are doing that.

**Story-guide:** What do I hear? What do I feel? I hear whisperings barely distinct, but I know that they are there, I feel excited that we might discover things. I also know that there are memories that occupy this dark place. I'll keep exploring in this way until you can join me.

**Story-guide:** What are you afraid will happen? My hand is waiting for you. Will you take my hand? I'm curious about the whisperings that I hear and the memories that are here.

**Story-guide:** Could it be that you are choosing not to remember?

After exploring this kind of difficult territory, it is imperative that you find a way to symbolically walk back together into the light of the here and now. Especially when you draw the session to a close, it is very important that you clearly make a move to come away from the darkness. You can do this, for example, by enquiring into – and highlighting if necessary – positive, affirming aspects of the person's experience. Please note that this is an 'advanced' choice of intervention and not everybody – neither Story-guide nor Story-sharer – may be comfortable with it. In certain cases, it may be the right step, but it is not one that should be taken lightly.

## The place for perturbance in intervention

In this model, sometimes the Story-guide needs to be in control of the pace and content of the sessions, planning carefully, rigorously reflecting and pro-actively perturbing the system where it is stubborn or resistant. Put simply, perturbance is about creating the conditions for the shadow behaviour associated with high stakes to emerge, so that you can actively work with it and help people change that behaviour.

Clarity about the purpose of perturbance in Story-work is critical, particularly in those moments when the going gets tough. For Story-sharer and Story-guide alike, there can be a fear of perturbance itself, or the threat of it. Even the mere thought of perturbing the root cause of the shadow behaviour can elicit fear of bringing on the dreaded symptoms themselves. This is all quite subtle and slippery but, if present, deserves your attention.

Comfort levels with perturbance often link to the Story-guide's own Story. Whilst any perturbance needs, of course, to be within your own tolerance levels as a practitioner, nevertheless, you do also need to be pushing and moving things. It is so much easier to step back and allow the Story-sharer to be in complete control, especially if you or they have such a tendency in the first place. Look out for signs of this phenomenon and when it shows up, actively work with it. Observing and noticing are important here, exploring when is it right to push and perturb, and when is it not?

> I think the biggest skill is in allowing the perturbance to just sort of be in the room and not rushing in to make it go away. There's all these things you can do to lower the tension; to ease the discomfort. But if you can, just hold it and let it sit as long as possible. Being clear about the purpose of perturbance is important too, along with the belief that something good will come out of it. You have to have some courage to do it and to hold people in the space and be confident to let it sit and simmer and be uncomfortable or have them be angry at you; then to sort of hold all of that lovingly. Love is kind of the wrong word but, in a way, I think that you need love. At least a certain kind of love that's – maybe it's more like a sort of deep empathy – for their wounds and their struggles and their struggling in the moment. I think you also need to have some sense of your own Story so you don't leap in, for example, to rescue. I think our patterns around conflict and conflict avoidance come in very strong. Or our patterns around vulnerability and expression of vulnerability or comfort or lack of comfort really show up in these moments so we need to be able to work with these.
>
> **Bridget, Coach**

There are times when the perturbance might be too much for the person, causing them to discontinue the work. This was Dan's experience when he found himself under-resourced in working with a leader:

> It's important working with this area to be connected to Self and to be authentic, in order to help build the container and create the right environment. I remember working with a leader and I misread his tolerance and the power of his Story. I thought some perturbance was in his best interests and it wasn't. He wasn't ready for it and he never came back. His partner called me to let me know how distressed he was and that he had fallen into his Story again. I regret that. It's quite a few years ago and I still remember it. That would be one of the examples where I suspect I did some harm; where I pushed somebody beyond where they were ready and I didn't read it. I wasn't in service - I misread what was possible and what was helpful.
>
> **Dan, Coach**

Below are some indicators of when there may be a need to be alert and delay any kind of eruption from perturbance:

- The context within which the Story-sharer is living and/or working is governed by a polite culture that dominates.

- Specific forces within the Story-sharer's professional or personal environment or context are determined to keep any mess from public view for self-serving reasons.

- A climate of fear acts to delay the development of trust in the Story-guide/Story-sharer relationship.

- The Story-sharer uses averting tactics to avoid any open conflict.

In the presence of any of the above phenomena, you need to be alert, but should still try to do what you can to overcome them. This is because the impact of the perturbance, when it happens, can turn out to be one of the most fruitful events in Story-work of this kind. It also signals an opening to go even deeper in the work and, in so doing, open new possibilities for change of a kind never previously envisaged.

# Chapter 7

## Go Even Deeper

### Resurrecting and redeeming the child within

*"When it is time for a new Story to emerge,
holding on to our past… only intensifies
our dilemma."*

**Margaret Wheatley**

## Why would anyone want to dig even deeper in Story-work?

Even when we have plumbed the depths of the childhood story, we may find it necessary to dig even deeper. This is because childhood stories, no matter how perfect, imperfect, turbulent or dysfunctional they may have been, are hard-wired into our psyche. They are familiar and entwined deeply within our identity. As we grow into adults the subconsciously emerging internal narrative accompanying the Stories also gets laid down in our neural pathways. It is not possible to make the Stories go away, but it is possible to integrate them in a sound way that says:

> *"Oh, that is part of who I am, the child who experienced what I experienced. I cannot make the childhood story go away, but I want those experiences to resonate in new and different ways."*

None of us would be who we are in the here and now, if we had not had the experiences we had. It is the parts of the experience that continue to haunt us and get in our way [through the internal narrative we have developed subconsciously in the past], that we are seeking to rob of their power, by bringing them out into the open. This is why actively gaining command and finding true peace with the Story through changing the internal narrative is the ultimate goal in Story-work.

*For me part of this was about being able to fight back, to say, 'no' – to Oppose. We had several conversations about how to do this e.g. Michael asked me the following question, 'Have you put in words and feelings something of what you need to say to your father before he dies?'*

*There were many twists and turns in the conversation, but overall what he was doing was seeking to empower me to fight back, helping me to realise the benefit of being freed up from that part of my past. Fighting back was about finding ways to finish up unfinished business on a promise that it would play a part in my putting the whole thing to rest. It didn't depend on my father letting me speak; it depended on me letting myself speak one way or another. I didn't need to be unkind to him, but I did have the right to fight back and do what I needed to do to like and love myself.*

*I resisted hard, but Michael made strong moves to keep this on the table. He was clear in his premise that if the goal was to put the past to rest then I needed to complete some unfinished business in myself in some way. The strategy my parents had employed had been successful in keeping me silent and what Michael was saying was, 'I want that child to speak through the heart of a compassionate adult.' I did this finally, finally in my father's last days as I sat by his side when he was dying.[10] [See Chapter 9 for more on fighting back].*

**Sarah, Author**

We tend to drag the Story of the child along with us into adulthood. It is as though the child comes right out front sometimes. We also know that the Story of the child, who in my case was denied real love and was injured, cannot wholly go away – in fact we do not want her to! We 'simply' want the adult's command of that childhood story and her internal narrative to change. And even as she changes the internal narrative more and more, the original Story will, of course, continue to lie at the core of who she is.

---

10 Obviously, one does not need to have one's parents alive to be able to talk to them, and to fight back. Ref: Hellinger Constellations and 'the empty chair'.

Questions about the childhood story and the old internal narrative will always continue to arise and, when they do, the Story-sharer can go back to:

> *"I know the origins of these questions, and they don't frighten me."*

As their Story-guide, you are looking for them to be able to do this with ease and then to make conscious discretionary choices in response. As a result, all the good things they denied themselves in the past, can become – at least psychologically – available to them in the here and now. Similarly, as they gain more and more control, they can start speaking with their own voice and are able to say:

> *"Coming out of my childhood story, this is who I am now, even though that child of the past is still there."*

By neutralising the power that the childhood story and its accompanying internal narrative had, by letting it go, the adult is eventually able to deal with the wounded child within.

> *The idea of letting go of the 'old narrative' sounded quite conceptual and abstract to me, but when I started to think about all the beliefs I held that were engrained so early on that I have no experience of life without them, it was quite unsettling. For example, 'I am completely unlovable when I am late; when I am upset; when I don't comply.' Those short statements, and many more like them, held power over me in unusually intense ways, despite being mostly sub-conscious to myself and completely invisible to others.*

> *It wasn't uncommon for me to move into a state of panic when I ran the risk of being late for an appointment. My heart raced, my palms became sweaty – a completely irrational response – and one that definitely not everyone experiences. It was driven by Story. Likewise, when I'm gearing up to disagree with someone whom I respect or care about, I can feel my heart pounding in my chest. And in terms of emotion, I would, up until very recently, have held back tears, even with those close to me, to the point where it was painful.*

*I knew these were not natural propensities – they went against the grain for me. They felt instinctively unnatural. Given free choice, I probably wouldn't manage to be rigidly on time, complying readily with what others said and expressing little emotion. For some, that may well be natural – but it wasn't for me. These were a set of rules that I had created to survive and thrive in my childhood environment – and there were many, many more. It was a form of Social Darwinism and it created a very specific frame for my behaviour, so engrained that it was easy for me to believe that others were playing by the same rules or, at the very least, could see them clearly and understand them – neither of which, I now realise, is true.*

*Breaking these internal rules was, and sometimes still is, very difficult. I had a lifetime of perfecting and putting them into practice. And a big uncomfortable question emerged for me on that journey – without these well-honed tactics, who was I? Initially, that was like staring into a deep, dark void. In times of change or turbulence, my experience is that we cling even more tightly to the familiar, regardless of the appropriateness and of the consequences. In some ways, that rather daunting part felt like a journey of re-discovery… who does the adult want to be now that she has free choice? An exciting question. And an equally overwhelming one.*

**Rebecca, Coach**

## Resurrecting and redeeming aspects of the childhood story

In entering the depths of the childhood story and its accompanying internal narrative, the diverse and complex ways in which the old and known 'ways of being' manage to stay in place start to become clearer. This is because there can be an implicit readiness in a person for aspects of their childhood story to resurface in adulthood, almost as if the person were somehow inviting them – even more so in the face of apparently trying to ward them off at the same time. In a sense, this is actually a clever – albeit somewhat distorted – way of coping with the threat of reliving past distress. The person sees it coming and pro-actively embraces the awfulness as a way of trying to deal with it, of taking responsibility, of making it less painful by convincing themselves that they are welcoming it; that they have some measure of control in that at least. This approach is understandable for a helpless, powerless child to take, but no longer appropriate for a healthy adult. Working on the childhood story at an even deeper level, creates the possibility to shake loose these old child-based ways of being, and to replace them with new pertinent behavioural choices.

> In the face of any kind of threat to me, I would be so ready to see, experience and open myself up to the threat, as a way of handling it, of at least keeping some measure of control. The person I perceived as threatening would not actually be doing anything harmful, but I would see signs that they might, or see something symbolically that might, and I would be ready to open my arms and take the blow. Psychologically, I was repeating the same thing I used to do as a child. I would get so disturbed by my parents' stress and aggression, especially in the way it would build and escalate over days and days, that I would go to a place of, 'Come on, bring it on, get it over and done with.' However perverse it may seem now, there was always a feeling of relief after the beatings.

> Fast-forward to my adult life. This was also how I used to go into a group as an interventionist, and there were some good things about being able to do that. I would feel and truly be very open. In fact, the more open I could be the more I believed the group could be too. I was open to whatever arose, including terrible things and would work productively with whatever would come my way from group members. It would be a way to manifest behaviours in the room and work proactively with those behaviours in service of the group. But rather than merely be in the room demonstrating how I could take the blows of the worst shadow behaviour, my Story-work helped me to do something much more constructive with my childhood story. I learned how to selectively let certain behavioural aspects into the room, but without letting them run roughshod over me and do damage anymore.

> I had carried into adulthood a very clever device and brilliant strategy to ward off a repetition of what happened to me. I became very sensitive to lurking

*abuse and readied myself for it. I could not defend myself anyway, so I might as well be prepared for it, at least I would not be surprised. And then I realised I could go further and actually invite it. I could make it happen, force it to happen on my terms, so that I thought I could – in a perverse sense – control it. The flaw in this was that as a child I started to feel responsible for making the abuse happen.*

*My next step in writing my new internal narrative was to tear up this concept of inviting abuse with its underlying hope of retaining some measure of control in this way. As an adult doing Story-work, I realised that this was not helpful and, in fact, by changing the pattern and not inviting abuse, I would not have to experience it anymore.*

*This change in the internal narrative also enabled me to redeem the child within, accept what happened to her, take the benefits of it and run with them, with me now really in control and no longer needing to open myself up to the next abuse.*

**Sarah, Author**

Once we have explicitly recognised and resurrected the impact of the childhood story we need to be able to turn it around a little bit. We need to redeem the child. Part of doing that means focusing on what we are doing and not on what the other person or people are doing to us. It is so easy to give others the power to behave in certain ways towards us, but it is incredibly hard to face up to the fact that this is what is actually happening and that we are collaborators. When we inadvertently resurrect aspects of our childhood story, we set ourselves up for failure and disappointment.

Strands of the Story may have resulted in us implicitly welcoming or inviting certain behaviours from others, even some of the darkest shadow behaviours, that were features of our worst childhood experience. Hard as this may be for us to accept intellectually, it also opens up the possibility for transformation, because, if we tend to invite certain behaviours, we also have the potential to rescind that same invitation. In other words, we can un-invite what we don't like and don't want. We do this by reframing and changing our mental models.[11] This provides one way in which we can begin to write our new internal narrative associated with the childhood story.

If something happened to you once, it can happen again. In this frame of mind, we let the damage in. If we change our mental model to include the notion of being able to invite certain behaviours, then it is absolutely possible to un-invite them too. This simple construct enables us to take command of our own behaviour and reactions to others. The paradox is, that we have the power to command what the child in us is afraid they cannot command. We really do have that power. As an adult, we can un-invite even the most shadow-ridden dark zone behaviours that trigger us.

The Story-guide needs to watch out for triggering self-blame in the Story-sharer as you enter or guide them into this kind of territory. In my own Story-work I felt really bothered by the notion that I was inviting the abuse or attack. The way I would show my annoyance would be by saying things like:

*"It's hard for me to hear those words . . ."*

*"I am not there yet . . ."*

*"I don't understand what you are saying."*

There can also be an obsessive quality to aspects of some internal narratives about childhood stories, in other words, they do not go away and they keep repeating. Rather than getting stuck on them, it should be seen by the Story-guide as a chance to pivot towards working with the Story-sharer on the feeling of being irritated with something about the Self.

## Holding on

Curiously, sometimes even after deep, deep work over an extended period, do not be surprised if the Story-sharer makes a last ditch stand to hold on to the dark parts of the childhood story. This is another manifestation of a person needing to hold on to those parts of their

---

11 In this context, 'mental model' is defined as our frame of mind or beliefs, ideas, images and thought processes about how something works, a representation of the world that surrounds us and how we perceive it.

Story. In a paradoxical way, for example, as in my own case, if the child takes responsibility and sees there is something wrong with them because of what happened to them, then they have a component of their identity that is what David Kantor [2003] calls a 'negative identity', and this is much harder to transform than a mere outdated internal narrative. In fact, the worst of all childhood stories is one where there is what Kantor calls a 'negative identity claim'. In other words, "I am that [e.g. worthless or unlovable], if I don't do that [e.g. put other people's needs ahead of my own]." Whilst we all may experience this to a certain extent in that we all have a story of imperfect love which says, "I am not lovable, if or when…" – with a negative identity claim this has become deeply embedded in our psyche and is both hard to shift and far from easy to re-write.

> Before starting the Story-work, in order to maintain my own negative identity claim about being worthless, I had to have the associated pain and the problem itself. There was a need for the negative identity claim, a perverse need based on my parents having 'convinced' me that I was unworthy and unlovable.
>
> How I got through this in the work I did with Michael was by talking with him about the ways I am loved and do love in my closest relationships. In connecting with these lighter parts of my identity, I could experience temporary relief from the darker parts that had been dominating my thinking and being for such a long time. What struck me through working on my Story was my positive identity and how it eclipsed the shadow side even if only temporarily to begin with. For a long time, there was a battle going on between my negative and positive identities. The work to do next was to stabilise the more positive aspects so that they could take over more completely.
>
> **Sarah, Author**

The slow, gradual transformation of a negative identity claim to a positive identity claim is a long, gruelling and hard journey that takes considerable time. This is because the negative identity claim comes from deep within the Story-sharer who has to negotiate numerous obstacles along the way. It is also a glorious endeavour and a truly extraordinary accomplishment.

*I know for sure that Sarah asked me on more than one
occasion if I could go back – go deep into my Story
and see the child as lovable. I remember sitting on the
phone in floods of tears saying, 'Yes, I can do that' and
trying really hard at the time to do so – I felt as if I should
be able to do that. I remember when I did first catch a
glimpse of the child [me] and felt a wave of love – 'Yes,
yes she is lovable,' I said. However, what I didn't say was
that it was fleeting. No sooner was I off the phone to
Sarah than I forgot all that was done and said.*

*So the next time, through yet another flood of tears,
Sarah was there for me again, this time with a variation
of her earlier intervention; 'Maybe there are some old
photographs you could look at and see how lovable the
child Nina was?' I agreed that yes there were, and that
I would take a look. I did – and chose one photograph
that my father had taken of me 'playing shops'. I did look
lovable and he had certainly captured something in that
moment. I guess that is why he took the photograph.
I hold that picture of myself often as a reminder of
that innocent, lovable child. I also had the pleasure of
watching, with my siblings and extended family, some
cine film footage – that again my father took – ranging
back to when I was only about one, up until about nine.
Wonderful to watch and witness in different ways how
much I was loved. These are really vivid pictures that I
can call up when I need to remind myself that I was and,
indeed am, loved and lovable.*

*Still, it did take several attempts and prompts from Sarah to
do this. I was reluctant I think to let go – there have been so
many times that in doing this kind of work on myself I have
felt on the cusp of something wonderful about to happen
and then it felt too scary to make a change and a shift.
What was different this time was the rewriting of my internal
narrative, which was helped by Sarah's encouragement to
reframe, to look back and see something different in the
child and imagine what a different narrative could be. I did
this through several cycles of retrenchment over several
years. At the same time, I was inviting my siblings in to talk*

*about several of the Stories we collectively shared. We all experienced the same thing and could almost verbatim hear my mother saying, 'Why can't you be like…?' We have laughed and cried about that many times, yet we have also found a way of understanding that, at the back of our mother's cruel words, she had her own Story; a story with my father, who had his own Story, and we began to understand that, in a strange way, she was trying to show love for us. She wanted the best for us, so she wanted us to do well academically and to 'stay out of trouble'.*

*She wasn't able enough at the time to realise that it was sending us in the opposite direction.*

*I try to remember as well all the wonderful things my mother had to say about me, and the wonderful things she taught me. Distancing myself from my narrative of being inadequate has been a piece of work though, and I had a bout of real retrenchment recently. But I could stand back and understand what was unfolding for me and, in doing so, I could work my way through it. The strange thing was that this time not only did I manage to Bystand myself; I was able then, after the tears, to laugh too, to see what had happened and smile. But the best is yet to come – I sat down to do some journaling and a new piece of the narrative emerged. What if I could really let go and imagine that I can be loved – just for being me, not in comparison to anyone else – just because I am me, what would be possible? I took this on and chose to live with that.*

*For me the change has been remarkable – I have found that I am indeed loved, just for being me, and it has liberated me in such a profound way that I feel better now than I have done in years. The more I feel I am loved as being me – then, as if by magic, I am loved; and then, as if by magic I am able to love and give more of myself to my relationships, both personal and in my work.*

**Nina, Coach**

Negative aspects of identity will never entirely go away, but they can be brought under control and diminished, so that they do not continue to do damage and do not cause the same anguish as they have in the past. Standing by someone as they go through this and seeing how hard it is, can be really challenging, but it is also good for the soul. It is glorious to watch the inner child arise out of the negativity that has dominated them. It can be hard to get there though, and in cases where an apparently intransigent, relentless negative identity repeatedly shows up, the person may require deeper therapeutic intervention, beyond the scope of Story-work presented here, and therefore referral to a therapist may be the correct course of action for you to take.

## Seeing things a bit differently

A paradox might show itself where the Story-guide takes an aspect from the Story-sharer's internal narrative and sees it in one way, whilst the Story-sharer doggedly holds on to seeing the same aspect differently. Take, for example, a descriptor of the Self as 'defiant'. It is possible to use this one single word in at least two completely different ways, one critical and one celebratory.

Being able to see things differently is an integral part of achieving the ultimate goal of creating a new internal narrative where the light is replacing the dark, and where we are reframing the negative. Central too, is the notion that when change starts to happen you might yet find that the person still holds out in the shadow. At that point, it is important to notice, if, when, and how fast they start to catch themselves following their old internal narrative and whether they can laugh at themselves in a positive way. It can be a sign that they are beginning to cast off some of the old disguises they have been wearing. It can also be a good indication that they are beginning to see and hear themselves in the present, and not be so swamped by their feelings or hooked by their Story and its old internal narrative.

In defining their new Self through the new internal narrative, it is important to guide the Story-sharer to reflect and enquire into positive aspects of themselves:

> *"What did I gain from those difficult experiences of the past, rather than what did I lose or what did I suffer?"*

> *What I gained was that I established a career in which I helped others to find their voice and in so doing, found my own. I achieved real clarity about how my childhood story*

*served me well. I also learned about how it did not, and what to do about that in those instances.*

**Sarah, Author**

The different ways the Story-sharer can build the new internal narrative are through:

- Recently developed personal and professional experiences.

- Letting go of some of the almost automatic [involuntary] behaviours of the past, [such as sacrifice of Self in order to compensate childhood experience by taking care of others].

- Being more balanced and measured about these impulses from the past.

The important thing is that through consciously writing the new internal narrative, the person will gain more command over their childhood story. This is especially the case, if they are alert to the fact that doing so with as much detail as possible will be the key to diminishing the ways in which the old internal narrative has impacted them throughout their life. Rebecca's experience at a residential workshop on 'Mindful Dialogue' provides a great example of what it can take to see things anew:

*At the workshop, I came face to face with my childhood story during an experience of being triggered by events that were taking place there. I felt out of place during periods of silence and in a context where we were practicing mindfulness and therefore connection with others was unlike anything I had experienced before. The silence was deafening. And so, I did what I did in childhood. I tried very hard to comply for a while, until such times as I could no longer, and then I rebelled. I became unruly and in a very childlike way, I became naughty. I allowed others to join me – and they did. In fact, as I look back on it now, it was a replica of childhood behaviour. If I wasn't 'in', then I would work to find happiness in being 'out' and that would be underpinned by a stubborn defiance, stark self-sufficiency and a definite spark of naughtiness.*

*As Sarah called attention to my behaviour through Bystanding and enquiring into what she was noticing, I heard in her voice disappointment, judgement and, whilst I can't remember the words, my translation was that she was telling me, 'You are being selfish. OK, you don't want to do the activity, but don't de-rail others.' It was the spark to my already well-built pile of kindling that said I didn't belong. I snapped. Publicly and aggressively, I played back to her that despite her preachings about this being a space without judgement, all I could hear was her calling me selfish. I was making a Bystand but it was laced with venomous Opposition. I then became quiet and withdrawn and despite the relentless efforts of others to engage me I would not be involved in the rest of the session.*

*As I left, individuals raced to comfort me. I wanted space and to be away from everyone but the desire to make it OK again was strong for some. Sarah on the other hand, stayed away.*

*As I reflected on what had happened, I realised that in that moment Sarah had been my parents' voice of judgement. She hadn't actually said the word 'selfish' at all. I had read between the lines. I had a Story in which I had, in my early teenage years, opposed a particular way of life and environment, which didn't allow me to be me. In fact, it judged me for being who I wanted to be, just like this environment appeared to be doing. Opposing it cast me into a form of social wilderness. And it had brought with it a raft of behaviours that I had found difficult to deal with. In this moment, they were being replayed.*

*I had worked with Sarah on my childhood story, she had been my Story-guide and we had subsequently developed a working relationship with deep-rooted connection. I began to judge, in fact, I began to blame her. How could she not see the motive for my behaviour was survival in an environment where I didn't feel there was space for me? One where my identity was neither accepted nor valued?*

What's more, I held the view that the participants who had joined me in what was a low-level form of sabotage, made their own choices. I was not responsible for them... I had, in childhood, often led others to join me in things we knew broke the rules for them to later abdicate responsibility with that well-known childhood phrase, 'well, it was her idea.' Even though that may have been true there was an abject sense of injustice and unfairness about the punishment that followed. And even without the overt accusation, my Story led me to detect the beginnings of an unfair attribution of blame, as used to happen all those years ago.

As the complexity of all of this swirled around me, Sarah kept her distance. I left the group and headed to my car, ready to leave. I was abandoning. Having abandoned the group's activities earlier that day through small acts of sabotage, I was now abandoning them physically. And then I saw it... the shadow of the Survivor. I was right in the middle of self-righteous abandonment.

Rapidly, the Story, the theme, the triggers and the sense of threat to identity all came into view. I hadn't seen them until now. I took the key out of the ignition. Right in this moment, I was a typology. One that kept repeating itself again and again, and I was tired of it. It had become predictably exasperating. This pattern of abandonment hurt other people, damaged relationships and prevented me from achieving some of the things I most wanted. Even though there was clearly collateral damage, ultimately the person who was most harmed by it was me.

And so I made a choice to do the antithesis of what I would normally do.

Despite every fibre of my body wanting to leave, I re-joined the group. I explained my decision to do so and shared my experience and my childhood story. I wanted the group, including Sarah, to understand why my reaction had been so explosive. It didn't excuse it. But it was my rationale. It was a Bystand of myself. In that moment, I believed I was at my most unlovable; a misunderstood child who failed to conform, disappointing those who loved her, only later to protest when she was castigated for her disruptive behaviour. I expected the group to superficially accept what almost felt like an apology and carry on about their day, talking about it in the margins when I wasn't present. Instead something extraordinary happened – the group expressed appreciation, said there was bravery in my sharing and that they felt honoured to have experienced what had taken place. It was the opposite of what I expected. It was the opposite of what the child experienced. This was the beginning of a new internal narrative being written in that very moment.

Sarah waited until the end of the session, then she came over to me and said, 'In this moment, you just became the teacher. And do you realise, I don't love you less when you have a high stakes reaction and behave in the ways you do, I love you more. I have never been more certain that you are capable of doing this work, not just for yourself, but with others.'

Despite the vitriol directed at her, Sarah had held that space, gently, lovingly and appropriately. There was distance and closeness in that moment that is so very difficult to describe but was so palpably felt. Had she been any closer she would have stifled, but any further away, I feel certain I would have experienced abandonment. It was a skilful tightrope walk, one without which such a significant realisation would not have been possible.

I remember that moment so distinctly because I think it was the first moment I was truly able to catch sight of the child and separate her from the adult. The adult chose a different response, the very first step on a long and challenging journey to write a new narrative. Rather than blaming external factors, which in all likelihood lay buried in her own psyche, she took responsibility. I would have expected the taking of responsibility for such a

*difficult interaction to have been awkward or bring with it*
*negative repercussions. Conversely, I remember feeling*
*enormously empowered.*

**Rebecca, Coach**

There is so much in Rebecca's account, not least of all the significant perturbance that was a critical part of the experience. Story-guides need to be able to sense when to move closer and when to step back in situations like this. They need to choose where to locate themselves. In this example, it was like standing on the periphery of the relational field to create and give space. It is also important not to stray into seeking to rescue the Story-sharer.

Rebecca had all the potential to catch sight of and change an aspect of her internal narrative that continued to plague her and yet it can be so easy as a Story-guide to inadvertently get in a person's way. The art is in metaphorically standing alongside the person even when appearing to stand at the edge. That way you can consciously hold the space for them and, in this case, hold it for the rest of the group who were also playing their own part in various ways because of what was occurring.

Through the perturbance and, most importantly, through Rebecca's own sheer determination and courage, she gained so much insight into the narrative she had been holding about this aspect of her childhood story. She began to see it in new and different ways. It was almost as if she was seeing things afresh through new eyes and, as she has brilliantly described, in those moments of seeing, her writing of the new internal narrative began in earnest.

## A grand adventure

To change the more stuck parts of the old internal narrative that grip the Story-sharer, consider asking them to have a conversation with their inner child; to literally, engage in a conversation with that child as a homework assignment. Even though this may seem like a slightly odd thing to do, when someone actually does it, things can happen that do not happen otherwise. Invite them to invent their own ritual for having a really open conversation. The goal is to enable them to separate themselves from the feelings that will inevitably be coming up for them about the child within. Ask them to create their own context for having the conversation, an e-journal, or paper diary should work well, as the writing helps with gaining emotional distance.

Inscribing the conversation, the pure experience of it and capturing it in writing is an important part of the exercise. The actual writing of it is very helpful, because it helps combat the impact of any overwhelming Affect that can manifest itself otherwise. It also makes aspects of the old internal narrative more visible and linear which means it can be worked with in a more logical way. The question or enquiry for them to begin the conversation might be something like:

> *"There are many openings here for change, what is behind the negativity I feel about myself and that appears to be blocking the change that could come?"*

This is one way of befriending the enemy part of the Self, the part that needs to be reconciled to be able to write their new internal narrative. In that conversation, the person can disagree with and challenge the fundamental premises that are keeping them locked in their narrative. The voice to use during the conversation is relaxed and gently wanting to know. In effect, the exercise enables the Story-sharer to make a friend of the Opposition again. Because there was once protection to be found in what is now getting in the way of them being fully liberated from the impact of their childhood story.

This is a challenging exercise and there should be no rush or pressure on the person to do it, because you are asking them to really look very deeply within themselves. The more you hang out with these darker issues in a genuinely relaxed way, the better and the more you will relieve any pressure the person may be feeling. Simply wanting the Story-sharer to succeed in generating an alternative to the harsher parts of the old internal narrative is also very important.

## Going back to the scene of the childhood story

Sometimes it can be helpful to physically go back to the location of the childhood story, to visit the origins of the toxic mess, to begin to inure the Self and detoxify the experience. I went back to the town I grew up in feeling curious, strong and clear. The best timing for this kind of visit is as the new internal narrative starts to emerge, as the person starts to feel different. It is a very good opportunity to test the difference. It is also a way of proactively working on the new internal narrative. This is because, in going back to the place where important events happened, the childhood story and accompanying internal narrative drags the person back into it. How well the person holds up under such an onslaught, is a good indication for how far they have progressed with the new internal narrative.

Overall, fortifying the Self with the creative struggle to define a new outcome is the work to do at this stage. It is not easy, but it is absolutely possible. The goal is that the person begins to really live the new internal narrative about the childhood story, and a visit to the scene of the Story is a great way to begin to gain command, because it enables them to put themselves outside the childhood story by looking back into it.

# PART THREE

*Change The Pathways*

# Chapter 8

## Don't Panic

### Commanding and changing the power of the Story

*"Any change, even a change for the better, is always accompanied by drawbacks and discomforts."*

**Arnold Bennett**

### Gaining more command of the Story

These last stages of deeper, longer-term work on childhood story involve finding ways to help the person gain more and more command over its impact in order to write a new internal narrative. Behavioural change is as much a desired outcome as a necessary part of the process. The childhood story and its accompanying [old] internal narrative will have influenced the person in serious ways throughout their adult lives, including, for example, in how they love, how they do not love and how they relate to Self and others. It is staggering just how deep and profound the influence of the childhood story can be. It is so powerful that it often successfully resists being transformed, hanging on by its teeth for as long as possible. It takes dedicated intervention and personal hard work to overcome the inner blockades thrown up by a besieged old internal narrative, before the time is ripe for the writing of the new one. This creation of a new internal narrative around the Story is a slow process. But it is an act of liberating the Self, of opening the locked gates, walls and bars that keep the person imprisoned in the negative impact of their childhood story.

> I have been working on writing a new narrative in relation to my childhood story. I think it's a slow process because I think you can intellectually know the Story, but you still have the reactivity to the situation that's reminiscent of the Story. So in the rewriting, you can have a different internal narrative, a rewritten internal narrative, but the rewriting

*has to be more like a rewiring of your reactions in the
moments where your Story gets triggered. I think that's
very slow work. I do. I have done a lot of work and it's not
like I don't react, it's that over time, I have a little more
distance from the Story and its impact and I see it a little
more clearly, and I see the connection to my reaction a
little closer to the time it's happening.*

**Bridget, Coach**

Inertia can also play its part in why commanding and changing the power of the Story and its accompanying old internal narrative is so hard. This is in large part because the Story-sharer has survived with it for so long that they find it incredibly hard to imagine life in any other way and see when things need to change.

At every stage, as the Story-sharer starts to turn things around, blocks and struggles can spontaneously appear, even though the person knows something good is coming on the horizon. They almost want to close their eyes to what is imminent, even though what is coming is good for them. Throughout the process of Story-work, the measure of ease in keeping the conversation about the Story and its accompanying narratives alive is very important, and is an explicit indicator of change occurring or being resisted. The Story-guide needs to stay engaged until the person gradually begins to feel more and more comfortable with talking about the more difficult parts of the Story, and light finally shines through the darkness.

### Fading the harsh resonance of the Story

There is a paradox in the experience of behavioural change occurring in this context:

> *"The fading out or changing of the adult-life resonance
> of the childhood story through the writing of the new
> internal narrative is both fantastically wonderful and
> incredibly stressful."*

The transition between the old internal narrative and the new one can be acutely painful. For a time, the old internal narrative is still present and may continue to be strong, but with the new internal narrative also already becoming more and more evident, albeit not as pronounced as we need it to be. This tug of war between the two competing internal narratives often results in the person being caught in a kind of no-man's land in the middle, for what can at times seem like an eternity. The experience can be of constantly moving back and forth between the two narratives, sometimes feeling intransigently stuck. Sometimes the movement takes the person backwards, and sometimes forwards. For a considerable time, what is familiar albeit disturbing – in other words, the old internal narrative – can still be stronger than what is new and empowering.

In an almost perverse way, the new internal narrative itself can also feel exceptionally hard to embrace. This is, in part, because of how it challenges and essentially invalidates the old one, which was with us for so long.

> I started to do new and different things. I approached things differently, made new and different choices and this all challenged the old narrative such that, for a time, it seemed to gain new strength and get bigger. There were several cycles of this happening and, during their peak, they were accompanied by considerable frustration and upset. It was a far from easy phase in the process.
>
> **Sarah, Author**

Do not be surprised if this happens. Really changing the internal narrative in a durable and sustainable way is a huge undertaking and is not easy. In fact, it is probably the hardest thing we can ask ourselves to do. Our internal narratives are stubborn, powerful, persistent and greedy. They are also domineering and therefore getting dragged back into the past is bound to happen. Over time, however, the impact that the childhood story has does change, and the recovery time from any associated retrenchment shortens [see Chapter 10 for more on retrenchment]. The important thing to keep in mind is always that we really do have full command of the choice to be in either world – a world dominated by our old narrative or a world according to a new and brighter one.

A valuable technique within this model which should be brought to the attention of the Story-sharer, is the amplification and magnification of the increasing freedom from the childhood story through the smallest of changes. Amplification often involves the Story-guide articulating the changes the Story-sharer is experiencing in an 'exaggerated' way to help the Story-sharer to see them. Eventually – supported by guidance and challenge from the Story-guide – there will be a shift from the old internal narrative and its associated symptoms having a hold on the Story-sharer, to the Story-sharer having a hold on them! Prior to this shift, you will see both narratives in-situ, which can be frustrating and confusing, but the arrival of even the slightest indications of the Story-sharer having even a temporary hold [conscious awareness] on the symptoms of their Story is such a good sign. When this happens, and as soon as you spot it happening, it is important to bring it to the Story-sharer's attention by holding it up and amplifying it so that they can see it bright and clear too.

## Don't panic if the old narrative reappears

As the internal narrative starts changing, aspects of the old internal narrative have a tendency to keep coming back relentlessly, and this can create real distress for the Story-sharer. Dealing with the most stubborn, deeply entrenched elements and the remaining bastion of resistance to letting go of them, can be very hard to work with for both Story-sharer and Story-guide. The quest for the Story-sharer, initially anyway, is to simply bring the moments when this resistance is manifesting itself, fully into their awareness. Awareness might not be sufficient, but it is an essential precondition to maximise the possibility for making different choices and reacting differently in those moments. This will not only give them a measure of control over their behavioural responses, but in some ways the very act of noticing that they have a choice can alleviate the suffering that often goes along with bouts of internal resistance and the resurfacing of old entrenched patterns.

> Instead of being a passive recipient of the internal narrative, I needed to Bystand [to notice or become aware] what I was doing to myself. I needed to step out and say, 'What I'm doing to myself in holding on to the negative self-image is pretty dumb and needs to be challenged by me! What kind of Bystander am I? I, the woman in there, dislikes herself and as a Bystander, this is exactly what I have to say to her!' This was so tough. It felt like torture at the time because I was so blocked and stuck, but it was precisely what was needed. Michael put me in the position of Bystanding myself over and over again and offered options for what that might be. It was

*like a battle between us and between the old and new*
*parts of the internal narrative. It was part of his role as*
*my Story-guide and it was what I had asked him to do*
*in working with me on my Story. In the midst of it all*
*he said, 'The girl will always feel like she failed, love*
*her anyway.'*

**Sarah, Author**

## Dreams arising as change begins to occur

Intrusive dreams do not only appear as the exploration of the childhood story deepens [as described in Chapter 6], they can also show up as change in the internal narrative begins to occur. Of relevance, is the notion that dreams which materialise in adulthood may actually have been childhood dreams. Bringing the childhood story up to the surface it is hardly surprising that the dreams of the past should appear too. When this transpires, it is helpful to look for any thematic structure in the dreams, especially when they are recurring. It is also important to watch out for the thematic structure of those dreams beginning to alter, as this can be an indication of change occurring.

An example:

Having had a dream about using super human strength to lift two demons up and throw them off a balcony, watching with satisfaction as they splatted onto the ground!

**Michael:** So how do you interpret the dream? What is the feeling?

**Sarah:** The feeling is of having taken control. We have talked about the experience of being overcome by another human being and this is the opposite of that. I felt strong. I felt that I could take this on, that I really could do something. I'm really moved and struck by how those experiences of having been overcome are still there. I don't know if this has ever have happened to you, but something fundamental is taken away as a consequence of being overcome by another human being. It's that feeling of having given up. I had all the shame of having allowed another human being to overwhelm me, to beat me to the point of giving up, of not being able to fight anymore. This dream feels like the beginning of healing that; the beginning of the new narrative in relation to it. The fear has been that I could be overcome again because I allowed it to happen back then. Let me correct that; it happened back then. I did not allow it to happen. It happened. I did not have the power and control then. I do have it now. And that is not to say that one day, I might walk down an alley or along a quiet road and something might happen – it could – but who knows what the outcome might be, it doesn't have to be the same. That's what I have been struggling with all these years, to heal that experience, that moment. It doesn't matter what was happening; it's that moment of giving up, of not being able to fight anymore and giving up. We talked about going deep into my childhood story being akin to peeling back layers of an onion and I've kept thinking I've got to the centre, however, I know now that this is what's at the core because it is so visceral. The memory has been trapped in my mind and body. It's released and set free now and that feels wonderful.

**Michael:** I think you have given a very clear interpretation of the dream that is your recovery from being killed.

**Sarah:** I thought I was going to die.

**Michael:** You know I was thinking as you were saying all this that there are so many people in this crazy, cruel world who are on their knees and there is a gun. In that moment, they surrender. A part of you was killed back then and in the dream you are saying, 'No, there is a different outcome. Miraculously, I can get out of bed, take command of the situation and do what I need to do.' The dream is about the next step in consciousness to reclaim what you lost and a sense of Self that is not subject to such threat. I understand in a sense better than ever, what you have been dealing with. We both should applaud the dream.

**Sarah:** [Through tears . . .] Yes.

**Michael:** Wouldn't it be wonderful if this were the beginning to the writing of the new narrative, if we could create a new path towards that?

**Sarah:** [Through tears . . .] Yes. It's time, it's more than time. I really want that.

**Michael:** I offer you my hand. My hand is there as you walk into the future with a new possibility of recovering from the experience of that moment of surrender. I love the dream. I just love it. It's got anger in it. It's got composure in it. It's basically got command in it. There are so many different things. We will come back to it.

At this point of the process, the Story-guide needs to use the dreams not to track back to childhood and what happened then, but rather to pick one of the things that was taken away from the Story-sharer, clearly identify what that was and then give it back to them. In doing this, you are transposing the loss and the suffering into something positive. The person then often starts to wonder about the behavioural patterns they have set up because of their childhood story, and when they are ready they will begin to make changes to those old involuntary and often harmful patterns. In fact, the change often just starts to happen spontaneously.

Perhaps surprisingly, as change at this kind of depth begins to occur, it can not only feel and be quite bewildering for the person, but also for those they are in relationship with. Altering well-worn behavioural patterns is not for the fainthearted. There are wonderful benefits, though it is not an easy path.

> In my case it was being able to fully take in the love that
> was so wonderfully given to me by my family, friends
> and colleagues. Through going to work on the writing
> of my new internal narrative I was effectively shedding
> or peeling off a strategy that I had maintained for a
> long time; which was to take care of others often at the
> expense of myself. Giving love had never been difficult
> for me but believing myself to be worthy to receive it and
> fully taking it in had been very difficult at times. Because
> of the new internal narrative in which I could connect
> with myself as 'worthy and lovable' I began to behave
> differently and this felt quite stressful to begin with. I
> was clumsy in many of my early attempts to change my
> reactivity and this was confusing for people around me

*who knew me. To deal with this, I talked with those who were closest to me about what I was trying to do and why. They in turn, did not waiver even once in helping and supporting me.*

**Sarah, Author**

Change for the better can also create stress and perturbance for the Story-sharer. This is, in part, because with the change there are expectations that they will feel and act and be better. But when it comes down to it, they may not be sure they can or even want to meet those expectations. There is an uncanny familiarity which brings a strange kind of comfort and security with what was laid down from childhood, including those familiar parts of the Self that are negative or even destructive in some way.

## Intrusive thoughts at night-time

Sometimes intrusive thoughts also show up on the cusp of change occurring. You do not want these thoughts to take on an obsessive quality, which they can do at times. The person then cannot stop thinking about an aspect of the Story and keeps replaying it in their mind. It helps to develop a pleasant ritual to counteract it, and bring the thoughts under control. If the Story-sharer is in control, rather than having their thoughts control them, they are more likely to be able to regulate the impact their thoughts have on them. It may seem paradoxical – and it is – but it is nevertheless important not to try to stop and suppress these thoughts. Suppressing never works, but gently guiding intrusive thoughts into a less compulsive direction can do the trick.

### *Activities that can help*

- Suggest they create a pleasant space for themselves by getting up, making tea, getting cosy and establishing a ritual for doing this, to be repeated each time the thoughts crowd in. The next instruction is that they sit down with a piece of paper and write the thoughts out. Writing them as a list form can be helpful – if you need to shop for the ingredients of a cake, you write eggs, flour, sugar, ginger… but after each item you stop thinking of the need for it because it's out of your head and on paper. In doing this, the Story-sharer is literally 'draining' the intrusive thoughts out of the mind, putting them down on paper and gaining greater control as a result. The person is making an explicit decision and action to take command of them.

- Be aware and prepared that the person will not succeed very well in trying to fight the thoughts, because they will just keep coming back. Instead, encourage them to ground themselves in present experience, which is under their control, and calm the thoughts, for example, using relaxation exercises or meditation, thereby starting to gain command of them. Mindfulness practice[12] is of particular value to achieve this mind/body state of being here, now, in this present moment, rather than being absorbed in unhelpful thoughts. Being present in the here and now enables us to pause to – for example – Bystand the Self and others.

Be sure to watch out for the person working too hard as a mechanism for counteracting intrusive thoughts. This will almost inevitably lead to exhaustion and serves only to create even more distress over time. You want them to sleep better, because they have a measure of control over their thoughts, rather than because they are completely exhausted from trying to control their thoughts.

## The paradoxical experience of change

A systems-orientated Story-guide or interventionist should remain a bit suspicious, alert to and curious about all data that manifests itself in interactions. For example, on the surface, support for the Story-sharer from others who are close to them may seem like a good thing. But there could also be other ways of viewing such demonstration of support that could potentially warrant further exploration. Sometimes the people around the Story-sharer, especially those who are very close to them, unconsciously or even consciously support the existing manifestation of the childhood story and the old internal narrative that accompanies it. They are, of course, then implicated in the system as it exists, but also impacted by any change as it starts to occur through the Story-work. This can sometimes help, but often inadvertently hinder the Story-sharer. These others too, will have their own interests with respect to how much they welcome change in their partner, friend or colleague.

One way to work with this is to ask the Story-sharer to consider and name the symptoms of the behaviour arising out of childhood story

---

12 Mindfulness practice as defined by Jon Kabat-Zinn [2016] is "Paying attention in a particular way, on purpose, in the present moment and non-judgementally…"

and old internal narrative explicitly as the enemy. Simple as this sounds, the Story-sharer might not be a willing follower to this suggestion. It might be necessary for you, as the Story-guide, to express clearly that you do not like what these symptoms do to the person; the stress it causes them, the drain on their energy and sense of well-being etc. You might also want to recommend that the Story-sharer actively enlists the people around them, their intimate partners, friends and colleagues, in the campaign against the enemy, i.e. against the symptoms of the behaviour. This is an excellent way to raise difficult issues in a blame-free manner with these significant others. The enemy is our own behaviour rather than another person we might associate with those behaviours ["You always make me react like this"]. The campaign is about recognising, 'owning up to' and eventually overcoming our own dysfunction, instead of a [revenge] attack on others for what they did to us. Andrew did this with his mother in a really beautiful way, and it went on to have an enormously positive impact:

> In terms of my own work on Self, I've been able to explore some of the internal narratives that I held closely, that to me absolutely were fact not fiction, and significantly impacted my behaviour for such a long time. I won't go into the detail of the Story, but one of the characters is my mother, and finding the courage, to say to her, 'Hey, this is the work I'm doing on Self, here's the Story that's come up, here's my lived experience of that, and here's the impact of that on me.' Not from a position of blame, 'How dare you?' but just, 'Hey, this is what happened.' From that, the most incredible unexpected thing happened; she then brought her lived experience through and there was a whole conversation around intent versus impact. She wasn't aware of the impact she had had and she was able to share some of her intent. So not only did I rewrite my own internal narrative about that Story, I actually rewrote it with her. Doing work like that, in such a critical relationship is incredible – the difference has been astounding. Before this, we would have just continued walking past it.
>
> **Andrew, Leader**

When our change meets our environment in the way that Andrew's did, the practical technique of explicitly and consciously naming our own behaviours as the manifest enemy means that the person has to take responsibility for their own behaviour. To do that, their energy needs to be directed towards the real opponent, their own dysfunctional behaviour and not the people who contributed to the behaviour becoming dysfunctional in the first place. Even if that is the truth, for example, even if Andrew's mother had brought this upon him, blaming her now would change nothing. Worse, it would keep him stuck in the old Story which cannot be changed, however often he revisited it. So unless he could change his paradigm, he would never be able to transcend that old wound – and because it was an actual wound, he couldn't ignore it either.

'Taking responsibility' is easily said, but it involves difficult and painful things. If we take Andrew's example again, before he could take real responsibility he had to let go of any anger and frustration about what happened to him, and the role his mother played in that. This was not for the sake of sparing his mother [although that would be a good side-outcome], but for his own sake, so that he could open up new possibilities. If he could not change his attitude to his past experience, it would always be a convenient excuse for any current dysfunctionality. After all, if he did not have a choice in his past experience, neither could he in his current reactive behaviour. Such wrong conclusions can have an iron grip on people. Logic never stood in the way of emotional distress and its long-term effects.

## Palpable turbulence of change

Curiously, periods of real growth can stimulate palpable turbulence for a considerable time. That things are changing and growing can be really challenging, no matter how much the growth is wanted or welcomed. This is, in part, because the shadow side of the Self sees only the shadow side of the change [the loss of familiar patterns], rather than the light side of it. As a Story guide you can construct and offer the Story-sharer plausible and useful propositions about the upheaval they are experiencing. It is helpful to be able to explain and give context to what's happening. There being anxiety about the change is only natural. We are so familiar with the old internal narrative that when things start to go well [and that means there is change going on] we get anxious about giving up something we have known so closely for so long. It is a very powerful paradox. It is almost like somebody who cannot leave an intimate relationship even though they are being harmed while they remain in it.

## Intervention example

> *"Have a conversation with the child within, revisit the experience you had and say what you are thinking, feeling and wanting to them. Know that they need compassion in this."*

In suggesting this activity, you are putting the person in a bind or a dilemma in relation to the child. This is particularly helpful when the Story-sharer is holding on to very negative, harsh or critical thoughts and feelings about the child. Name what you are doing and maybe even say to the person:

> *"You are wrong and mean to blame the child in the way you are. The innocent child needs to be loved. They did not deserve what happened to them."*

To really help the Story-sharer lift themselves up out of the darkness of the internal narrative emanating from their childhood story, they need you to be undaunted. Do not let them push you away. They also need you to be elated with them when you sense that you are on the right track with them, even though they may not be able to see it themselves yet. This will serve them well as you guide them into the next stage of Story-work where they become increasingly proactive in the creation of new pathways and in pursuing the writing of the new internal narrative.

# Chapter 9

## Be The Author

### Creating new pathways and writing new internal narratives

*"The big question is whether you are going to be able to say a hearty 'yes' to your adventure."*

**Joseph Campbell**

### Changing the realms of what has been invisible

Freedom to dance in the streets comes from the writing of the new internal narrative, making public the idea that something has happened that we can celebrate. This is not just a personal victory. For there to be hope in the world, it is necessary that there be examples of people who take an experience of imperfect love from childhood, carry it into adulthood, and then put up the fight to change the impact of the Story. This is how change can truly happen, for the individual as well as for society. We not only affect different outcomes for ourselves, but also for the health of our social systems by doing this work. Individuals who are no longer controlled by harmful narratives make for a healthier society. They encourage healthy growth and become moderators for escalating high stakes situations which otherwise easily get out of hand.

The child within us needs to be known and witnessed, to be known and witnessed again, and known and witnessed, yet again, after that. This is what happens through doing deep Story-work. There is usually a sense of profound and pervasive misunderstanding in our lives when the inner child is not known. A kind of voice saying, "You don't understand!" which is the adult trying to express an inner dilemma:

> *"I can't reveal the child to you, I am too scared to do that - but what is happening here is causing real distress to that child which is a core part of me."*

During the process of Story-work, we will come to a point where we know enough about the childhood story. We can then start putting it in perspective and concentrate on treating it for what it is – a factual, yet isolated event of the past and neither a determinant of our present, nor an oracle of our future. Having lived – mostly unaware – with our Story for so long, there will be things we have taken from it, things that have shaped us, things that we need to bring to the fore and become aware of... so that we can make – for the first time – a conscious choice of what we want to carry forward, and what we want to leave behind.

Sometimes, this process of seeing the Story for what it is can manifest itself in a tiredness with the old internal narrative and a readiness to move into the new one. It feels like there is suddenly an annoyance with the old behaviours, thoughts and feelings. The same old behaviours, thoughts and feelings we previously desperately wanted to be seen and heard so much. Now that we are increasingly at peace with it, we are getting bored with its annoying appearances and repetitive repercussions. Hallelujah!

There will always be moments of tension [high stakes] where some aspect of the childhood story and the accompanying old internal narrative gets triggered and comes back to the surface. That is when we can relish the real triumph of Story-work, because now we are in command of our dark forces, we know them, we know they are still there, we know they will rise up from time to time, but they no longer have a hold over us.

> I feel very at peace with my childhood story. I have acknowledged very much what it is. I still find myself reacting and responding. I lose my voice sometimes. I get scared of speaking up, but I'm very conscious of when it's happening and now I tend to go, 'Oh, that's interesting, OK,' but I don't give myself a hard time for not pushing through it. It's alright. It will come when it comes and that has helped a lot. It's a lovely thing to look around the room when you're nervous and think, 'Everyone has got a Story of their own here and they are all struggling with things in their own way.'
>
> **Ann, Director**

The new internal narrative can have astonishing healing powers. It can heal the pervasive and persistent infestation of bad feeling about the

Self. As noted previously, if we do not feel compassion for ourselves then the ancient wound from childhood continues to fester and simply cannot heal. The writing of the new internal narrative is the turning point. We are on to a different outcome, because the new narrative is far from mere wishful thinking; it becomes the foundation for a new reality filled with possibilities. It actually happens through the work done between Story-sharer and guide. The Story-guide provides the alternatives, the new possibilities, modelling them through what you do together during Story-work. What emerges is an altogether different kind of internal narrative. An example:

## The Story and its old internal narrative

> One day one of the boys she hung out with had taken her to the railway line that ran through the fields about a mile away from their houses. He forced her to play 'chicken' on the railway track making her stand on the line and not move until he told her she could do so. She could hear the train coming and then saw it turn the corner approaching her. She was shaking violently, crying and begging him to let her move. After what seemed like an eternity he dragged her off the line, just in time. He was a bully, he would force her to do things she did not want to do and she would just seem to let him. She was 9 years old. He was 14. Long after that day she would return to the railway track by herself. It was as though she was returning to the scene of the crime where she had experienced such terror. She would stand there on the line just to feel something, just to feel alive. She wished she were brave enough to stay there, to let the train mow her down. She felt like a failure for not finding that courage. She was in search of peace. She existed in numbness; it was hard to feel anything very much.

## The new internal narrative

> What an extraordinary thing she did in returning to the scene of the crime. She was so smart and so brave, because rather than shoving what happened underground as a terrible action and pretending it didn't happen, she found her own brilliant psychological and

*sometimes paradoxical way of dealing with that awful
reality. She played out the scene again of daring death,
because she was feeling bad and, in so doing, she felt
more alive. She truly was wonderfully courageous.*

Writing the new internal narrative grows out of the struggle with the old one. It opens up the possibility for us to set a new course, to move forward on a new path, to diverge – if ever so slightly at first – from where we orbited before. Where things go next, it does not matter. What does matter is that it is not the path of the old internal narrative. It is a new one, and it will be a better one.

## Dealing with entrapment in the old internal narrative

Parts of the old internal narrative can get activated again and again in the presence of people closely connected to the childhood story of the past, such as, parents, siblings or other family members. This is because they may be directly implicated in parts of the Story. There can be strong feelings for the Story-sharer, such as guilt or shame, frustration or anger, or even concerns about disloyalty to the 'old system'.

*Some of the disturbance I felt was around 'disloyalty'
and the challenge of implicating other loved ones in
the experiences I was sharing. It was so hard to explore
this, but I found it so helpful as a construct to be able
to accept that some of my childhood story was real and
some of it was perceived. My perception was of course my
reality, but understanding this gave me a permission to
explore it a bit more.*

**Rebecca, Coach**

The feeling of responsibility can show up in many ways. It can be expressed in relation to the 'old family system', including anybody who played an abusive part in their Story, and those who were not abusive themselves, but appeared to let it happen. There can also be a strong feeling of responsibility for a new and better inclusive narrative which does justice not just to the Self, but also to others. Abusive as the person might have been, they had their own suffering and limitations, and they also had their own childhood stories.

There has to be a place in the new internal narrative for those people who populate our old Stories, whether they are alive or dead by now.

So long as the Story-sharer stays in the Stories of those others, as an object in their Stories, rather than as the acting [commanding] subject of a new internal narrative, the power of shaping the future is lost to the Story-sharer. They are somewhat in a trap then, but they can get themselves out of it. They simply have to internalise the notion that they have the option to take back command of their lives, through writing their own new internal narrative; a narrative which is governed by them, where they are the central character, rather than the hapless object of others' whims.

In practice there are, however, a number of different possibilities for dealing with entrapment in relation to a particular character featuring in their Story:

- Keep on struggling as before, against their own psychological interests, with unease, angst and often worse suffering being a constant presence. In effect, do nothing. Doing nothing is a valid option even from a Story-guide's perspective, but knowing that it is the Story-sharer's choice is very important.

- Rise above it; in other words, be so removed from how they really feel about that character that they can act with a different spirit. For example, the person might be able to treat the character in more generous and understanding ways, locating empathy for them, Bystanding in Meaning when they are with them. In other words, generally employing methods for lowering the stakes for themselves and others.

- The final, and perhaps most preferred option, is for the Story-sharer to take a position of only doing what they really want to do, and no longer complying with what they do not want. As part of this, the person consciously begins to say "yes" to authoring a new internal narrative relating to these characters. The new narrative is literally lived and written at the same time. This can be embodied in the following statement from the Story-sharer: "My new narrative now separates me from you." With the new internal narrative, the person has the agency and the capacity to leave behind any prison and torment that their past saddled them with.

   *No one was fighting to have custody of the ten-year-old boy as his parents split up. Abandoned to the fate of a boarding school and passed around friends of friends during the inconvenient holidays, he knew what it was like to be on the receiving end of indifference. The abandoned child in adulthood had become an expert Survivor adept at abandoning others and in a career that allowed him to move on every couple of years, conveniently ensuring no one got too close to him! Imagine my surprise, having done deep work on my childhood story to suddenly find myself, the 50-year-old adult, caught up in the childlike behaviour of seeking the attention of my father. As I found myself being rejected over and over again I was being pulled towards the relief of abandoning my relationship with him altogether. The abandoner was looming large, but this time I knew it, knew I had choice and knew I had a new narrative that separated us. I chose to be for my father the father he hadn't experienced – available, offering unconditional love and empathetic. I had struggled with it, tried to rise above it, but ultimately the change had to happen in me and as I found ways to embody my new narrative I freed us both...*

**John, CEO**

### The business of authorship

The knowledge that they have the right to their authentic emotions, and do not have to go through in-authentic ones to please others, is crucial for the Story-sharer. As they are authoring their new internal narrative, the Affect [what they feel] becomes clearer and is no longer muddled by history. This is evident even at times of directly touching upon that history, for example, when they are talking about family members, because how they are talking about them is different; it becomes solid and that bodes well for the future. If those historical Story-characters are still alive, how they are talking to them can also become more solid. There can be a different quality to these – formerly difficult and awkward – conversations. Others around the Story-sharer might start to notice the difference too.

It is important that the Story-sharer does not hold on to any historically loaded expectations of family members. But, at some point, the Story-sharer has to decide whether to make their family aware, both of their distressing [if not outright disturbing] experience of them, as well as of the work they are doing to create a new internal narrative in relation to their childhood story. At times, remarkable though it might seem, this decision about sharing or not gets taken away from the person; they may find family members spontaneously initiating a conversation with them about things they are noticing about them. Family members may even already be behaving rather differently towards them as they sense that something has shifted. As the Story-guide, it is important to emphasise that the change – while manifesting itself in the new and different behaviour of others – is located in the Story-sharer. We are dealing here with a cascade of change, starting in the Story-sharer, whose impact on those around them is changing, and therefore the reaction of those around them is changing too.

Sometimes, in the process of writing the new internal narrative, people do need to do or say something to a family member or a character in their Story, in a sense to react as an adult in ways the younger child could not have done. For the Story-guide it is important to raise this as a possibility or as a question, and to ask:

> *"What do you think about that? Is there anything you need? Do you need to reconcile parts of your history through conversations with ******?"*

It is important not to press for this kind of clarification or reappraisal if it does not resonate with the Story-sharer. Most importantly, the Story-guide needs to be clear that we are not talking about taking revenge [on any of the Story-characters] here. Revenge is the least helpful thing that could come out of doing Story-work. Any direct engagement should be neither maudlin pleading nor vengeful mauling, but with a focus on informative assertion of who the Story-sharer is now, what journey they have behind them, and what they are capable of. There is some hope that the other person – accustomed as they might be to their dominant role under the old internal narrative – may take notice and realise that they do not have this power over them any longer. But in the end, it does not really matter how the other person reacts. The mere act of taking an adult stance towards a formerly intimidating Story-character, is an act of liberation and personal growth.

## Fighting back

Fighting back – in the way I am describing it – is a big thing psychologically in the writing of a new internal narrative. Its purpose is to help the

Story-sharer in finding ways to say to whoever may be triggering the Story or be implicated in it:

> "I am in command of the Story in which the child in me got harmed."

The intention is to detoxify issues arising out of the childhood story, especially around particularly important Story-characters.

> The physiological reactions I used to have to the merest mention of my father or references even to the name of a person whose behaviour seemed harmful to me showed me two very significant things. First, the degree of my reactions demonstrated the power these figures still had over me. My reactivity was still destructive to me and – hard as it was for me to accept – I realised it would remain that way until I could do something to detoxify my issues and in so doing, change the internal narrative. It also showed quite clearly the power my childhood story still had over me and I knew I needed to get to a place where this high level of reactivity didn't keep happening. The consequences of not doing so would be that the pattern would simply keep on repeating and re-manifesting as it had been doing for years. This is where the notion of 'fighting back' proved helpful.
>
> **Sarah, Author**

One way to 'fight back' is to write a letter to the people in the Story with the purpose of using the writing of it as an exercise in 'fighting back'.

> This is what I did – eventually – but not without a fight! The path towards putting pen to paper was rocky, to say the least. I really challenged the point of writing the letters. I was belligerent in my view that there was no point, because my father was never going to read them and, if he did, I believed that nothing would change and it would risk making things worse. I knew that my father didn't have it in him to respond differently and join me in my writing of my new internal narrative. I had tried many times before and he had shut me down every time.
>
> **Sarah, Author**

Sadly, sometimes there are people who are simply impossible to reach emotionally. Finding a way to 'fight back' then becomes even more imperative. It is also possible that characters from the Story may already have died, leaving behind issues that remain unresolved for the Story-sharer. Writing a letter to such unreachable people can be a great process for assisting the Story-sharer in moving forwards, in just the same way as if the character were emotionally accessible or still alive. However, self-doubt and fear can be strong blocks at this point. Facing resistance to a suggestion of this kind, it is helpful for the Story-guide to offer a re-frame, for example, from:

> "I don't think I can do it" to "I don't think I can do it at this time."

The resistance in itself is not a problem, it is merely a symptom, which shows that the hurt child within the adult is still present.

> Over time, with help, what I came to understand was that there was something important just in the act of writing even without sharing it. This was because I grew able to see how writing could play a part in diffusing the power that the experiences with the aggressors in my life were continuing to have on me. Separating the child-Self from the adult woman was the goal. This was not to dismiss or bury the child's pain or to make the child's Story go away, but to free the adult from the effects in the present.
>
> The writing of the letters was part of the whole process to understand the girl, to understand what happened to her and to diffuse the effects on the child-Self that remained in the adult, but also to give the adult woman more freedom to live and to do her work. I could put the childhood story in a separate place and work on it at the same time. It meant I could work on what was getting to me, what was still hooking me, what scared me, what humiliated me and what I could do about all those things. I knew well what the child went through, but could separate the links to the present, and this meant I was successful in doing the transformative work that I needed to do in order to fully love people that were important to me.

*I was also professionally able to deal with a much wider and freer range of behavioural options. For example, at that time I was working with a couple of police groups where I was encountering very strong and stuck Opposers. In the past, I would have allowed this pattern of behaviour to trigger me into high stakes and tried to stay safe by backing off. I actually found myself able to step forward and make different interventions, which enabled me to respond differently and hold my ground in a constructive way. I haven't looked back since!*

**Sarah, Author**

## How to write a new internal narrative

### Connect with the potential

It is critical to have an eye on the full potential of the new internal narrative from the outset. With that in mind, in practice it helps to begin by exploring where the person is being haunted by their childhood story and searching for signs of this manifesting in the here and now:

*"What is the link between current, observable behaviour and Story? Is there one?"*

*In my own Story, self-doubt was so evident even in the early sessions, and the exploration route we took was to illuminate the extent to which the self-doubt I was expressing in the here and now [and even in the coaching relationship itself], was actually springing from self-doubt seeded in the past through an aspect of my childhood story. We needed to know that part of the Story. We also needed to make sure I didn't get stuck in it by dwelling there too long so we moved back and forth between the here and now and the past in every session.*

**Sarah, Author**

It is important to keep bringing the person from the Story back into the present. We cannot resolve anything in the immutable past, but we can deal with the present directly and overtly, and, in so doing, we are beginning the writing [or rather the enacting] of the new internal narrative. In other words, we explore the dilemmas and troubles of the past, but we especially explore their impact on the present. This helps us see the potential and promise of what is to be gained by healing the wounds from childhood. It does not miraculously make every dysfunction in us disappear instantly. But noticing and becoming consciously aware is a crucial first step.

## Learn to love the child

It can be truly difficult to unravel the ways in which the child takes responsibility for parental cruelties and other harm. However, if this attribution to Self continues into adulthood, the adult cannot love that child inside, and so cannot love the Self. The point of Story-work is first to get the adult person to love their inner child just the way they are, and then to separate the child from the adult. Only when this is successfully done is she ready and free to write the new internal narrative.

There can be many recriminations by the adult towards the inner child in their Story – being weak, responsible for what happened, disgraceful, loathsome, etc. Recriminations towards the inner child may also show up when the external world – in its own dysfunctionality – appears to affirm our deep fears, for example, that competency is absolutely vital, and love is contingent on winning. Whilst asking someone to learn to connect and love the inner child in their Story sounds so eminently possible and easy, it can feel like torture for the Story-sharer. Even the merest suggestion of doing so by the Story-guide can create a visceral reaction. After all, who would want – or even be able – to love such a flawed, bad, wicked human being. And here lies the crux; obviously our image of the inner child is not a realistic one. It is deeply flawed and distorted, yet we hold on to it desperately and against our own interest. Overcoming this is such a critical step in the process of locating real love for the inner child and being able to write a new internal narrative.

> *I had a habit of overburdening myself by saying 'yes' to too many things and taking on too much, going too far with things. Now being able to say, 'Well yes, but not now…' or asking people to wait and if they could not do so, knowing and believing that that really was OK. I used to fear that I would not be loved, if I turned people away, so I would just keep saying 'yes' to things. The changes I made here were another example of fighting back. 'I like myself enough that I can risk you even going away rather than just saying 'yes' and, in so doing, overburdening*

*myself.' This was another way in which I was able to move forward in the writing of the new internal narrative. The experience of letting love in, really letting it in, was absolutely wondrous.*

**Sarah, Author**

### Locate empathy and compassion for characters in the Story

Another important part in the process of writing the new internal narrative is enabling the Story-sharer to locate empathy and feel compassion for people that either hurt them in their childhood story or influenced them so significantly that they still hold on to behaviours that are damaging to them, in the elusive hope they will be loved for this eventually. This helps the Story-sharer to lower the stakes for themselves. The beauty of compassion is that it enables you to neutralise all the power that those from your past otherwise have over you. Locating empathy and compassion does not have to rule out the possibility of you being angry, disappointed or sad – at least temporarily – for the choices others made and the way they behaved. What compassion does though, is free you from the hold others and your experiences with them have on you. This is the best part of compassion.

*With my own parents, I was able to see and connect with the reality that they had their own childhood stories and I came to understand how these played out in their lives and in the way they had behaved towards me. To the extent that they harmed me, the best way for me to rid myself of that harm was to understand their Stories compassionately.*

**Sarah, Author**

Equipping leaders with a range of mechanisms for locating empathy and compassion for the people around them, especially for those who trigger them the most, is really liberating. Rather than blaming another person who may represent some kind of nemesis to them, can they try to connect with the fact that this person has a childhood story too? They do not need to know what that Story is precisely, but they can make up an approximation based on their experience of this person. This opens up the possibility for letting empathy and compassion in, which in turn reduces the stakes and creates the potential for a much broader range of responses, suddenly at the disposal of these leaders in the new low-stakes environment.

*As the newly appointed CEO of a large organisation I was astounded at the personal accounts that were tumbling from the mouths of people about how the previous leader had shouted, bullied and even physically injured people over a ten-year period. Although now on the sidelines, he was still exerting significant influence over others and I later realised this included me too! He just wouldn't get out of the way and let go. It seemed like long tentacles from outside were swirling around in the system and implicit criticism was having a voice in the media. He had truly become my nemesis. I had nearly burnt myself out blaming him for his behaviours and impact on me!*

*When, through the work I did with Sarah as my Story-guide, she helped me find a place of peace about the change I could undertake in myself, amazingly the problem seemed to evaporate away! Equally significant was when I constructed a narrative about his childhood story from the behaviours I saw. I couldn't know if this was true, but it helped me to instantly locate empathy for him. The compassion I found for him transformed me, not him. No longer in high stakes at the merest mention of his name, I was free to access parts of my leadership that were previously being swamped.*

**John, CEO**

## Strengthen and expand the behavioural repertoire
A critical question in Story-work is:

> *"What do you do with the original experiences, with your actual immutable childhood story, which has such strength and impact on your behavioural options?"*

You don't want them to go away. And, in any case, you can't make them go away. They are indelible. Consequently, the best alternative is to say:

> *"No, this is part of my identity, so then, what are my options?"*

The options then become the way in which your immutable Story affects your behavioural choices. What you as the Story-guide can do, is to work with the Story-sharer to expand their behavioural options, such that they have more behavioural choices. What gets transformed is not the original childhood story, but where they take that Story into the future. As such, all that we deal with in Story-work can be used to strengthen and expand a person's behavioural repertoire.

An example:

> Referencing the cruelty I suffered as a child, I explored what part cruelty played in my adult life; the extent to which I was especially sensitive to it, and the potential downside to this sensitivity in my professional and personal life. For example, before I did Story-work it was easy for me as a professional to misread Opposition as being cruelty, which would then impact on my choices of intervention and could render me disabled in the room. There was also a risk that I would soften my interventions for fear that someone in the room might experience something I was doing as a form of cruelty. The goal in changing this was to get on the other side of this fear and add to my repertoire so that I could stand firm in the room when faced with people who were inclined to cruelty [the Fixer heroic mode in the dark zone], especially when I was the target.
>
> The new internal narrative was akin to viewing myself as a potential expert on the complex phenomena of cruelty and its effects on people. Within this, I needed to be able to do my own version of fighting back to the cruelty, and I needed something that would take me over the line of politeness and discretion to fight for something good. For that, I needed to expand my behavioural repertoire, not least of all in consciously choosing not to be so much a Protector [heroic mode] steeped in Affect that I would get lost in that part of other's experience at the expense of other dynamics in the room. I constantly asked myself, 'What might I be missing through holding onto this old internal narrative? And what do I need in order to grow?' In this case, 'What might I be missing by holding onto an old internal narrative that all Opposition is cruel and reacting accordingly? And what

*do I need in order to become more skilful in reading
the room for healthy Opposition and responding more
appropriately to it?'*

**Sarah, Author**

The old experiences from the past form an integral part of a person's identity. Through Story-work this identity starts expanding now as well. Thus far it was chained in by the original experiences. Now when the chains come off, the person suddenly has so many more options as to what to do with their basic identity. I firmly believe in the possibility of using our very worst experiences for something good. Story-work gives us a clear roadmap for how to do this. In a sense, Story-work professionalises our human instincts. As Story-guides we encourage and enable the people we are working with to really become masterful at putting their childhood experiences to rest and emerge the stronger and better for it.

## Don't try too hard!

It is vital that the Story-sharer does not get stuck in trying too hard to find solutions for the pain of the childhood story to go away. It is worthwhile emphasising, yet again, that the childhood story does not ever go away, and that – strangely enough – one should not even want it to. After giving due consideration and effort to the characters and plot lines of the past, it is the triumph of taking back personal freedom from what happened back then that really matters. You don't have to resolve your past, it is enough to transcend it, as discussed earlier. Trying so very hard to resolve the past is a kind of trick on the Self; it is present and future relationships with people close to us now that are more important than the people, family or parents that populate our Story from the past. The people who are close to the Story-sharer now can become the very antidote and remedy to the grim haunting of their psyche by the ghosts from the past. It cannot be stressed enough how important it is for the Story-sharer to celebrate what they have achieved despite their history. It is time to revel in their potential in a future freed from the shackles of their own mind-trapping old internal narrative. The earlier they can make that shift from brooding [too much] over the past, to engaging [insightfully] with the present, the better.

Trying too hard to make the childhood story go away can have exactly the opposite effect and keep it right where it is, because the excessive focus feeds and preserves it. It can be painful for the Story-sharer to hear this, especially if they have done a lot of work previously to cope with their history; to really work at it, and to try to make it go away. Unfortunately, the 'process of trying' to deal with the past, and working so hard on it, can have its own contorted benefits. It typically gathers a lot of people around the 'struggling person', people who love them, who are sympathetic to their plight. Those same people would, of course, be close, even if the person were not trying so hard. Unfortunately, this can be hard for them to believe or accept. The big question of "Am I lovable?" is always lurking in the background. The very act of doggedly trying what cannot possibly be achieved in the first place, will naturally become exhausting and depleting eventually.

The proposition of not trying so hard to make the Story go away can also seem dangerous to the Story-sharer for fear of getting hurt, because the trying hard in itself can be a defence against the danger of being hurt again. The work of the Story-guide – when this is presenting itself – is to find a way to convince the Story-sharer that giving up their defence and bringing an end to trying so hard will in fact not condemn them to eternal suffering, but lead to redemption for the inner child.

### Accept there will be fear and confusion

As the new internal narrative starts to emerge, the experience can seem dangerous. We suddenly find ourselves facing the prospect that something different could happen, and this can be scary and confusing. How on earth could you give something up [your old internal narrative] that – at least as far as your inner child is concerned – has saved your life? Well, let's say you do not have to give it up, but you should move it aside a little bit and make room for something new, room for new behavioural choices that will help you live a full life now, rather than trying to ward off torments from the past.

Don't worry about confusion. The confusion, the questions and doubts surrounding and besieging various aspects of childhood story, do not ever go away either. Doubt represents the grip of the past. Like the Story itself, doubt about the Story will not go away. What happens through Story-work, though, can best be summed up thus:

> "You get to smile at your doubt, even when it has you in its grip. It's a matter of what you do once you know the Story very deeply, what it is all about, and therefore what your new internal narrative for your adult life will be."

The job as a Story-guide is to create the conditions and space for the internal narrative to be written and fully taken in. The childhood story needs to be scrutinised and probed inside out, but without drowning in it, as we have emphasised before. When we can finally engage with, comment on and see through the Story with all its twists and turns, it is a sign of having finally arrived, of being in command of the Story and ourselves.

### Integrate and share the new internal narrative

How do you know when a person has written a new internal narrative or has laid aspects of their old childhood story to rest? Quite simply, they do not think about the childhood story so much anymore and when they do, it does not impact in the same hefty way it used to. It just does not have a hold over them anymore. Their adult Self is no longer the figure or character from their Story. They have successfully repositioned themselves [their adult Self] in relation to the historic character [the inner child] in their Story. They have become both actor and author of their own new Self. They are in 'full possession' of their Story, they are in command of their Story [and their Story is not in command of their behavioural reactions] and their Story is integrated into their leadership.

> When leaders can come in and openly share their childhood story, if that's the right thing to do, it's incredibly powerful because of their willingness to express vulnerability and be authentic about their high stakes leadership behaviours. It's about them saying, 'You know what? Leadership is not always about being perfect. It's not always about knowing the right answers. It's not always about being the most stoic, stiff-collared executive you can be.'
>
> **Mark, Coach**

By sharing the Story, the Story-sharer literally strips away its cover which was originally set in place to hide it [and thereby preserve its power]. The more integrated and comfortable you become with your Story, the easier it becomes to selectively share what you need to share with people close to you, like members of your family and colleagues. Those around you start to see the changes in you as you do the Story-work; and these will be changes for the good. The process may not be easy, though, and there can be times of distress as things unfold. The people around you will also get to see the not so good aspects of you doing your Story-work. This, of course, leads to a range of possible reactions in those around you, from urging you to stop, all the way to urging you to keep going.

How a person integrates their achievements during Story-work is a key part of the change that comes with writing the new internal narrative. A question like the following is helpful in exploring this:

> *'How close are you to being able to give up responsibility for the dark and ugly parts of your history and take in the love you earned?'*

### Celebrate the victories

Do not forget each one of the good things that are happening, as they are happening! Keep them in sight. Any victories over the dark side of our behavioural patterns along the way should be celebrated, whenever they happen. Don't strive for perfection before you enjoy your progress. Acknowledgement and celebration are an important part of changing shadow behaviours. Acknowledgement and celebration of the new identity that emerges out of the past Story speeds up the work in progress.

In a similar vein, as a Story-guide you need to be particularly alert, observant to – and not inadvertently ignore, or even disparage and belittle – what people have already accomplished in triumphing over their childhood stories and dark behaviours before they started Story-work with you. Acknowledge and celebrate all of that. Remember, too, that the dark shadow side can, of course, also get in the way of enjoying the celebration. This also needs to be worked on.

### An intervention for co-authoring the new internal narrative

For the Story-guide to be an effective co-author of the new internal narrative, you need to know the full script, and you have to be willing to work closely with the Story-sharer. You might even co-design interventions based on the specific needs of the individual Story-sharer as they are arising in the process. An example:

> *My goal was to get to the point of doing as much as I wanted to do in the care of my father. I needed to get to a place where I could make the kind of judgements about*

*this, free from my childhood story. Even though he was becoming frailer and frailer, I could not have known at this point, but I did not have much time left to achieve this before he died. What unexpectedly unlocked things for me in extraordinary ways was the use of pictorial images to tell the Story and communicate something of that to my father. I needed to go slowly with this and take one step at a time. It would have been so easy to choose an image of a powerful male figure looming over a child conveying the powerlessness I felt with him when I was small. Instead, with Michael's guidance as we co-designed this process, I chose to tell the Story using images of fathers and children connecting with one another, with obvious love in the exchange. The images of the children conveyed calmness and security, connection and love.*

*Looking at the positive images of daughters and their fathers was poignant and impactful. It highlighted the beauty of the relationship between a parent and child and connected me powerfully to the lack I had always felt in my relationship with my own father. It touched the loss and absence of that and I really allowed myself to feel the deep sadness I had been staving off for so long. It also connected me to the accompanying appreciation of the wonderful love I have received from other deep and loving relationships I have been blessed to experience in my life.*

*Instead of focusing on the negative and engaging in the spirit of maudlin victim with my father, the aim in my account was to start by picking images that depicted a child's right to a story of perfect love. The reason for doing this was to help me come around to the idea of myself having the right to have perfect love. This was a critical part of writing my new internal narrative. I no longer needed to relive the loss and pain. I was ready to move on to better pastures – and let my father know it.*

**Sarah, Author**

When making interventions [using pictorial images or similar] to co-author a new internal narrative, it is important to slow down the pace and guide the Story-sharer to choose the images carefully. The stance is one of working together to find the right way to convey the Story. Be ready for potentially strong reactions in the Story-sharer as they engage in this activity. This is a perturbing intervention out of which profound change can materialise. Strong feelings such as anger may emerge. As these feelings manifest themselves, important and good things can happen, triggered by and within this process of co-authoring the new internal narrative.

## A tug of war

There is a contrast between the old internal narrative and the new internal narrative that becomes more and more apparent as the new internal narrative starts to take shape. The feeling is one of being more in command of the childhood story, more equipped to deal with moments when the old narrative shows up uninvited again, knowing how to look at it, and having conscious ways of dealing with it. Along with being in command of your Story comes real strength, and that feels genuinely positive.

There can also be a tug of war going on between the old internal narrative and the new internal narrative, and at times it may seem like the old one will simply not give in. It can be as though the old internal narrative is brave and spirited, almost fighting for its right to exist. This is the most difficult part of change itself. It is the reality of how powerful the old internal narrative is, and how hard it holds on to the person. As we write the new internal narrative and essentially an obituary to the old, it is important to realise that the old internal narrative can only have less strength and less hold on us, if we truly accept the underlying Story as an integrated, sorrowful, yet benign, part of ourselves and do not fight it. Those experiences happened: the only thing we can change is their impact on us. Whatever it is they induce in us, that is what we need to put an end to. At the same time, we need to get familiar and comfortable with the whole idea that we will never get rid of the childhood story, and instead focus more on how we can recast its formerly debilitating effects into positive ones.

## Hope comes in, but wait . . .

You want the Story-sharer to get on board regarding the need to detoxify themselves from the power of those very negative feelings about the Self. In the process, you will begin to discover what appropriate next steps towards detoxification might be, and you will come up with suitable next moves together for writing the new internal narrative. The subconscious fight of the inner child against change and progress becomes weaker and weaker. Although, along the way towards the new internal narrative, the old one keeps popping up and causing problems, a bit like an uninvited 'trouble maker'. The resistance may still be there; it can be felt, but it gradually stops blocking us in the same forceful way it did previously. Things that seemed impossible before, now suddenly seem possible.

As the Story-guide you will be able to tell that the Story-sharer, through the Story-work, is evolving in very observable ways. You will be able to experience this change in the sessions with them. You will gain wisdom and insight as you dig deeper into the childhood story and uncover more of the old internal narrative. It can be confounding to realise that, even after extensive uncovering of the Story, the old narrative is perfectly capable of staying in hiding [perhaps in plain sight] and needs to be teased out tenaciously. However, the reward makes all the efforts worthwhile. As you decipher your old narrative, you can feel a sense of real hope and possibility emerging.

> On the other side of your childhood story, there is more hope than you can even begin to imagine at the start! I knew that I had needed to go back to sort out the mess of the childhood story, but one day I also realised that I no longer needed to keep going back in the same intense way that I had been doing for such a very long time. This moment was so important. I was finally the author of my own new internal narrative.
>
> **Sarah, Author**

However, then, just as you think you are nearing completion of the Story-work, do not be surprised if the Story-sharer comes to you with the last shackle of the old internal narrative, asking you to join them, yet again, on their journey of discovery, before finally drawing the work to a close. This may refer to a deeper aspect of what you have already been dealing with. They may be asking you to go even deeper with them, or it may be something they have not felt able to share previously. Whatever it is, you need to attend to it. It might well be something akin to separation-anxiety, where the Story-sharer has grown used to the Story-work with the Story-guide and feels anxious about the prospect that the process – however successful so far – is coming to an end.

## Final battles and Story setbacks

Yet again, even after this final piece of work, and as you believe the Story-work is actually drawing to a close, do not be surprised if you find yourself in a closing battle.

> *One day the intrusive impact of the abused child was really gone. She was no longer operative in me in the way she had been before. My past had been a living nightmare at times, but at last it truly was in the past, where it belonged. But not so fast! Suddenly, I found myself putting up a final fight, and I staged a battle with Michael about it. I was still holding on to the last vestiges of the Story, and he was challenging me to let go of these, because the change truly was taking place. Subsequently, I had a nightmare and guess what? The nightmare dragged me back again and in so doing, the purpose it served was to perpetuate the old internal narrative. Thankfully, I toughed it out by painstakingly going back over all that I had learned, and with Michael's help, was able to get back on track with my ever-growing command of the childhood story and ever-evolving new internal narrative. Actually, once I was out on the other side of it, I realised it had been a fun and necessary fight. It was a part of the writing of the new narrative.*
>
> **Sarah, Author**

A change of this kind is such a significant achievement, but still no reason to let complacency creep in beyond this final stage in the Story-work. This would be a dangerous thing, because even with the best of wills, and the most insight and skill available, when truly high stakes are brought about [by our very own special personalised set of triggers], that old internal narrative will still at times rear its ugly head. We will find our sensors lighting up like a night sky filled with the flames of rocket fire, and before we know it, we will be acting out of our shadow once again. All the elements of high stakes reactivity we have worked so hard to transform will be on full display again. Do not be disheartened. This is a life's work.

> *I would say, 'If you get triggered, pause and voice it if you can, because the high stakes will diffuse, if you can name them. Catch who metaphorically entered the room and*

*watch them leave again!' The writing of a new internal narrative is never-ending work. It's necessary and it can be fun to do too.*

**Aidan, General Manager**

Knowing and understanding what our high stakes triggers and themes are helps tremendously, and Bystanding the Self in Meaning can calm even the strongest waves of emotions and associated waters of despair. Every time we get triggered again, as we surely will, know that we have not gone backwards. Paradoxically, this looping-back actually represents yet another step forward in our process of redemption. What matters most, is not a perfect record, but rather what we do next with what we have learned. There is more to come for sure.

### How to write a new internal narrative

*A summary*

- Connect with the potential.

- Learn to love the child.

- Locate empathy and compassion for characters in the Story.

- Strengthen and expand the behavioural repertoire.

- Don't try too hard!

- Accept there will be fear and confusion.

- Integrate and share the new internal narrative.

- Celebrate the victories.

- Expect a tug of war.

- Don't be disheartened when the old internal narrative re-emerges unexpectedly.

- Trust the looping nature of Story-work.

- Embrace the set-backs.

# PART FOUR

*Walk Your Talk*

# Chapter 10

## Hold Out Your Hand

### Cultivating closeness, love and reciprocity between Story-sharer and guide

*"Come to the edge, he said. We don't dare to, said they. Come to the edge, he said. We are afraid to, said they. Come to the edge, he said. And they came. And he pushed them. And they flew."*

**Apollinaire**

### Holding out your hand

It really matters if your hand is held when you are in pain. The brain is affected differently if someone you trust is holding your hand [Ackerman, 2012]. The Story-guide holds out their hand to the Story-sharer:

*"Know that I am with you, I am standing alongside you, supporting you. I am holding out my hand to you."*

Learning how to feel love, really take love in, and bathe in its glory can become possible through the deeply nourishing relationship between the Story-guide and Story-sharer. As a Story guide, you really come to know the Story-sharer. You begin to see the full picture of who they are and what they have experienced; you really get who they are. That puts you in a unique position to help them confront and work through issues in their childhood story. You will know that you are on the right track when you can almost feel how you are coming to know the person and their Story more and more deeply.

Coaches, however, often get confused on the issue of their relationship with clients, and its closeness and emotional connection. The extent to which you choose to connect with the client will depend on your Practice Model. For some practitioners, the stance is that there should best be no emotional connection, preferring instead to take an objective and neutral position in the relationship. In contrast, in the model of Story-work presented in this book, it is a good thing for the Story-guide to develop a rich relationship built on deep knowing of the Story-sharer and their very personal childhood story, including the nourishing care and support that is a central part of that.

Trust is the bedrock of all relationships, and it is certainly no different in Story-work. The Story-sharer entrusts themselves and their Story to the Story-guide. The surest way to ensure that trust can emerge is to be transparent, to be open, and to ask questions immediately as they arise. Knowing another person deeply and exhaustively is in itself a profound experience. Knowing someone on such a profound level is a form of love, and this aspect is very important to the relationship that builds through the exploration of the childhood story [Kantor, 2012].

The importance of loyalty and healthy attachment to the person you are working with cannot be overstated. The Story-guide needs to be a solid and loyal companion to the Story-sharer, a fierce Survivor and Protector who will not allow that loyalty to be shaken by the inevitable doubts and confusion of a struggling Story-sharer:

> "I'll show you; you won't wear me down. Just you watch me! It is the way it is between us."

This is what the Story-guide needs to convey consistently in different ways.

## Closeness, dependency and reciprocity

There is also a certain kind of emotional closeness in the relationship between Story-sharer and guide. Why shouldn't the Story-guide want to take care of the person, be there for them, engage with them? Therefore, because this relationship is so central for the process, and a very close one, attending mindfully to the relational boundaries is a critical imperative. The Story-guide may symbolise many things to the Story-sharer, such as a good parent or a good friend. The unfolding connection can often be touching and tender, with a certain kind of reciprocity in the relationship. The giving and receiving does not have to be one-sided. The Story-guide is receiving too.

*It's pretty intimate when you go more deeply into childhood story territory with someone. I feel very connected to the person and the sense I often have is that I will do so for life. The coaching may be over, but I would be so thrilled or honoured just to see them. It's just like you've entered some entirely different level where you really start to connect. It feels very powerful.*

**Bridget, Coach**

Sometimes a worry can surface in the Story-sharer that the relationship and the sharing is too much, potentially leading to an unhealthy dependency. If present, this is an important reflection for the Story-guide to detect, to bring into the open, and to explore with the Story-sharer. Over time, as the Story-work progresses successfully, the outer expression of the childhood story changes and the adult Self of the Story-sharer becomes stronger. Initial concerns that the relationship might be counter-productive, or that the request for help is too much, often simply evaporate as the process unfolds. We literally can see the person in the telling [and through the telling] of their childhood story becoming stronger and stronger.

In my own work as Story-guide, I often orientate myself around this issue of dependency by assessing whether there is genuine movement, and whether qualitative differences are noticeable as the work progresses. Of course, people get stuck from time to time. That is only to be expected. What I am gauging is whether, overall, there is movement of some kind. While this is happening, I don't worry about dependence. I rather see whatever is taking place, as the necessary building of an important, close relationship that reaches to deep levels of 'knowing'. This relationship is in service of the Story-sharer, liberating their voice, and brings an end to the intrusion of toxic elements driven by an outdated internal narrative that is negatively impacting their adult lives.

## Does love exist? If so, is the love real?

Love between the Story-sharer and guide is both real and not real. Real love is characterised by its slow growing nature, its unwavering commitment, its profound depth, and its palpable impact. That kind of love is present in the Story-work relationship. But because of the usually commercial arrangement in which the Story-sharer is paying a professional fee to the Story-guide, it might also in some ways seem not quite real. However, if we use David Kantor's definition of Love as 'a form of deep and caring knowing', this makes the love in Story-work real, because of how deep the Story-guide gets to know – in fact by definition of their role must get to know – the Story-sharer. On the other hand, because the Story-sharer – also by definition – cannot know the Story-guide in the same way, the love between them is not – and cannot be – as real as in other constellations. This is another set of paradoxes to be aware of and to be worked with, if questions or concerns arise around the theme of love and its role in Story-work.

Like all paradoxes, this can be really confusing for both the Story-sharer and the Story-guide. I know that I personally have felt real and deep love for people I have done Story-work with, and they have often expressed their love for me too. I have not been directly asked this question, "How real is the love in Story-work?" But I did ask it of Michael, my Story-guide. I think this was largely because love had been such a central theme of my own Story-work, and how he had used himself in service of me writing a new internal narrative for myself in relation to love. His answer, "It is real and it is also not real", was perplexing to say the least until I understood it more clearly.

Conventional wisdom within the therapeutic world says that love in this kind of client-practitioner relationship is not real, that it is just a form of transference that needs to be analysed and got out of the way quickly. David Kantor, however, says that the nature of love is a universal phenomenon, and that nobody has the answers to what the nature of love should be in any relationship, whether it be therapeutic, collegial or between intimate partners. In a way, he rejects the notion that he must get rid of the thing that people would call 'transferral love', just because somebody invented this negative label. Unfortunately, a lot of professionals mess things up, precisely because they do not talk about the issue of love. In this model of Story-work, love needs to be talked about explicitly, as the theme arises. Starting with a proper definition of love would then be a good start, combined with an awareness that there seems to be an obsession with romantic love [whatever that is supposed to be] in our society, to the exclusion of anything else, especially to the exclusion of a proper understanding of what love is in the first place.

One other way that the love during Story-work is reciprocal, that it goes authentically both ways, is when the Story-guide reveals their own imperfections. It is in the nature of Story-work that the Story-guide is assigned worthy qualities by the Story-sharer, but this is not demonstrably earned. That said, it has to be that way, because it is through the 'magnificence' of the Story-guide that Story-sharers allow themselves to grow. Being valued and really known by a magnificent, 'more perfect' person is a strong commendation and motivator. Because the Story-guide will most likely come to be viewed by the Story-sharer as almost 'perfect' in some way, it is important to name that naturally there are imperfections too. However, when the Story-guide tries to reveal themselves as a real person with all the imperfections this entails, this can break the spell or inadvertently reverse things. That we as Story-guides are imperfect is certain for sure. The Story-sharer therefore needs to know that the Story-guide has imperfections and limits too. They do not need to know about them in detail, but they do need to be reminded that we naturally do have them. The context for the Story-sharer needing to know about the limits of the Story-guide is that this is a part of being in service of their Story-work. What really matters is the struggle together to make sense of the Story, and the relationship which is forged by this shared struggle. It is all in service of the Story-sharer and their journey to bring about change through the writing of a new internal narrative.

Know that sometimes the person working on their Story needs a trustable parent, sibling or friend, and you may represent that in some way to them. Talk about it openly. Work with a professional [Story-work] supervisor too. Deep knowing leads to compassion and love, and you will, of course, get to know the people you work with in this way. There is nothing wrong about this. Be simply genuine and authentic and respect the boundaries. Use the relationship to help the person to get to a better place.

Love between the Story-guide and Story-sharer – of the kind I am describing here, and as distinct from romantic love – is acceptable, because it is manifested in an appropriate form, with very clear and explicit boundaries. It does not violate the moral core of the other. There is much fear about this topic of love and transference in the psychoanalytic and psychotherapeutic territory. This is largely because of concerns about boundaries being crossed, for example, through the development of a sexual or intimate relationship. Being appropriately in role with one another is of the utmost importance in Story-work as in any other coaching setting. The conversation about the relationship needs to be kept open and the Story-guide must ensure that there is sufficient space where questions about the relationship can arise, especially if, at any point, the feelings which Story-guide and Story-sharer impute to each other are getting in the way of their private or professional lives. In the event of this happening, stopping the Story-work would be recommended.

## Place and purpose of retrenchment in Story-work

The Story-sharer never needs their guide more to hold out their hand to them than during inevitable retrenchment. The inescapable crises and periods of retrenchment that arise during Story-work can be really useful in deepening the exploration of the childhood story and redeeming certain aspects of it. When something comes up in the process that throws the Story-sharer off balance or pulls backwards in some way, it is important to withhold judgement, because it is what you help them to do with the experience that really matters. Retrenchment is inevitable, at times frustrating, even exhausting, and yet useful. It always has the potential to be the basis for a bigger leap forward, even if in these moments the Story-sharer may well doubt the gains they have made and may well need reassurance about the place, purpose or impact of retrenchment. Safe in the knowledge that it is possible to make something good come out of the retrenchment, it is our role as Story-guide to infuse the Story-sharer with confidence and trust to continue their journey.

The symbolic role of the Story-guide as a caring individual in these moments of retrenchment alongside the person who is struggling with their childhood story can be mixed. In joining the Story-sharer during these difficult moments we evoke the past with all its suffering. Being associated as Story-guide so closely with the harrowing distress of the past, may test the relationship between Story-sharer and guide, especially if there has been abuse or abandonment in the childhood story. The Story-sharer may challenge the guide in the following ways:

Q: *Are you really there?*

Q: *Do you really care?*

Q: *Did you really mean it when you said you would support me?*

All kinds of doubts and defences can come to the surface. This is neither surprising nor extraordinary. It is another form of retrenchment or regression. There is always a likelihood of temporary retrenchment, and this means for both the Story-sharer and the guide that you simply stay with it, and you go back to the Story unafraid. Retrenchment is a necessary building block of successful Story-work. It serves a purpose. It is painful for the Story-sharer, but it is a necessary step to progress to the next level of growth. Ask the person to lean on you as the Story-guide throughout retrenchment, and reassure them that there is no reason to be unduly concerned about this. It is the way real change happens in Story-work.

A personal experience to illustrate:

> A crisis of retrenchment struck me like a tsunami hitting land. As I finally came up again for air from the depths of the ocean waves, I felt battered and bruised as I desperately searched for a lifeline to grab hold of. I turned once again to Michael for help and, in the same way he had done on so many previous occasions, he extended his hand to me without hesitation at the very moment I reached out to him. In the palm of his hand lay the centrality of Bystanding in Meaning, which he repeatedly and unequivocally offered to me as the ultimate of all lifelines for moments like these.

> In that moment of crisis, it had been so hard for me to receive the help he was offering, because to do so I had to overcome the intransigent power, strength and pull of my treasured Affect that was coursing through every fibre of my being, and which kept dragging me back down beneath the surface of the water. It was as though I was drowning and battling to come back up for air. So what exactly was I fighting for or against?

> I was fighting a known, but oh-so-powerful internal narrative of the past. The Story lay in the seabed, which was thick with silt and seaweed and littered with sea monsters lurking in the shadows behind jagged rocks. My wrists and ankles were bound by the tendrils of the old internal narrative associated with that Story, which were clinging to me like an indomitable force dragging me back into it.

*This was a fight for survival, but not in the way you might expect. I knew the actual Story of my personal survival all too well. This was different. Here, the old internal narrative itself was fighting for survival, and to my absolute dismay, this time it was winning. After all, I had worked hard to gain command of that outdated internal narrative in my adult life, but none of that seemed to matter now. The hooks of the old narrative were sitting deep and it was fast winning this battle.*

*I felt weak in my fight towards freedom from the shadows of the childhood story and I retrenched into abject separation from everyone around me. I disappeared inside my Self; an old strategy that had always afforded me some safety in the past. I had felt my resolve weaken as I continued slipping and sinking into the dark ocean of the Story. No heart there. Letting go. Slipping away behind my eyes, headlong into the depths. No room for others. No space for love. Presence suspended. Slipping further and further away. It's like I had become the shadow. I was the shadow. The familiarity of the feeling of separating my Self was both agonising and horrendous.*

*I found the experience of retrenchment to be such a poignant and tough one to endure. I was able to function but suddenly my thinking and decision-making were shaped more by the old internal narrative than the new one and, once I caught sight of this, I felt so distressed. No matter how deeply Michael and I had worked together, equipping me with all the insight, skill and process imaginable to gain greater command of the childhood story of imperfect love and its effects on me in my adult life, I was suddenly confronted with the reality that there were extraordinary powers out there that could undo any gains I had made. It was a critical and tender moment as I recognised how rapidly the old internal narrative had regained lost ground, completely taken me over and swamped my sense of reality, of trust, of all the big things we had worked on. I was devastated by the shadow part of the Story taking such an easy hold over me after all the work I had done.*

*With a combination of Michael's help, unstinting support from those closest to me, and my own resilience and strength, I dragged myself up through the density of my distress. In doing so, I was suddenly compelled to face up to the notion that I was still vulnerable to triggers that evoked my Story, and to acknowledge all the mess I could potentially still create [for myself and others] as a result. How responsible was I then for controlling the impact of my Story, when there were things that were powerfully and involuntary triggering me? My answer? I was and always will be absolutely responsible for my behavioural choices even when those choices are more limited because of a triggered crisis. How could it be any other way?*

**Sarah, Author**

The combination of, and connection between, Affect and Meaning in doing work on childhood story is a critical theme. In the eye of the storm – around what I had experienced as a betrayal of trust by a close and trusted colleague and friend – what I had needed most was Affect. Essentially, I needed Michael, metaphorically and maybe even actually, to throw his arms around me, to comfort me, and to reassure me that all would be well. All this, before moving towards Meaning that his own behavioural profile so readily gave.

It is a curious dance. The introduction of Meaning really can help someone high in Affect to lift themselves up and out of the intensity of emotion, especially when it has become unproductive and threatens to overwhelm them. But in a high stakes situation for the Story-sharer, a well-timed expression of Affect by the Story-guide can be the very thing that prevents an escalation into the murky territory of shadow behaviour. In addition to the importance of keeping the right balance and sequencing between Affect and Meaning, the expression of too much Meaning by the Story-guide can be received by someone high in Affect, as disconnected, cold and unfeeling. This can make it even harder for the [high Affect] Story-sharer to get grounded, stay connected, and ease out of the grip of the Story and the distress it is creating. That said, it is always a vexing question how one can really know when and in what form to best reach out to someone in Affect – or anyone for that matter – whilst they are in the grip of their Story, in the midst of an emotional storm. To do so risks sharp rejection and outbursts of more

Affect. On the other hand, not to do so risks creating fertile grounds for further entrenchment of the Story-sharer into the feeling of being unloved and unlovable, particularly when this is a critical theme in their childhood story.

The complexity of Story-work is never more visible than when the Story-guide has dropped into their own childhood story too, because, of course, Story-guides always have their own Stories. Why wouldn't they? We all do. And why wouldn't they have needs and flaws too? Why wouldn't they suffer from being involuntarily triggered, and as a result exhibit their own shadow behaviour? When both people are in their Story, sparks can fly; collisions can happen; devastation can occur. We each seem to want to drown out the other person. We become fixed on the Self when such escalation occurs, unable to see the other or to really connect with them. Driven by deep-seated old narratives, we are both lost in our own inner reality, which largely remains invisible to the other.

The job of the Story-guide is, in fact, to help the Story-sharer see how wonderfully beneficial retrenchment can be and often is. Crucial learning can come from it, because of what it can enable us to see, because of what it can reveal as it takes us – potentially – to a wholly different level of insight. A skilful Story-guide will help us reach a place where we can be thankful when retrenchment occurs and appreciative even for the pain that it causes. Retrenchment and how we cope with it, is such an important phenomenon. When things feel as messed up as they do during retrenchment, it is important to recall that it actually is the blatant visibility of this 'messed-up-ness' that is so valuable for the process of Story-work.

Of equal significance is to always remember the importance of love, of Affect, and of the need for reassurance. Reminding the Story-sharer that being lost in retrenchment is not a permanent state, that coming out on the 'other side' will happen eventually, and that greater strength and wisdom lies there. The intense vulnerability within those feelings of loss and confusion so common in retrenchment should be fully acknowledged and witnessed, rather than be ignored or missed for the sake of a predominance of Meaning.

> *"Sarah, I promise you we really are going to learn from this and I'm not going anywhere. I'm right beside you."*

*Michael's words restored my Affect in such a helpful way. I think because at last he was offering me some reassurance. Some hope that I could, and would, come back from the separation from Self that I had learned all too well as a way to keep myself safe when I was a child. That I would get through the pain of the retrenchment and that something really good could come of it. He was showing me, yet again, that we were in this together, that he would not abandon me in the way I had been discarded and let down by my own parents repeatedly in the past.*

**Sarah, Author**

## Identification between the Story-guide and Story-sharer

As a Story-guide, knowing your own childhood story well and how it manifests itself in your adult life, can enable you to identify faster, better and deeper with key aspects of your clients' Stories. This can be remarkably helpful. With the ability to rapidly and acutely identify with others can come the feeling of being steady, present, content and at ease to meet people where they are in their own Story. It allows you to be bold, brave and authentic in doing truly excellent work. There can be an absence of fear for the Story-guide in these moments. However, identification with the Story-sharer can also come at a cost. Identification works in two different ways. On the one hand, you understand the Story-sharer in ways that others cannot, but on the other hand you also, because of the identification, absorb some of the Stories in ways that others do not. They have armour that you no longer have, because 'identification' has taken away your armour in these instances. Both effects of identification intensify your experience with the Story-sharer. This can lead to exhaustion easily. You may do your best work as Story-guide, but it can leave you feeling completely drained.

Another aspect of identification is that you may miss what is going on for yourself during the process, because of your own self-neglect. How many practitioners do really make sure they have the necessary supervision and support in place when they are doing this kind of deep work? Unfortunately, there are very few outside of psychotherapy, where it is considered malpractice not to have such support mechanisms available. A serious Story-guide should always have a supervision arrangement in place, if only to check in regularly that truly no supervision is warranted for a given individual.

David Kantor also warns us about 'leakage' of what we do and do not do in our personal lives into the work we do with Story-sharers. He emphasises, "Watch your words!" It is one thing to draw on your experience and own Story in service of the Story-sharer, but there is a fine line between constructive sharing and inadvertently messaging something that is more about you and your own struggle with your internal narrative. Also, be careful that you do not inadvertently reinforce or amplify a part of the Story-sharer's narrative in an unhelpful way, just because it somehow resonates with your own Story and narrative.

## Turning the tables on you

Watch out for the moments where the Story-sharer turns the tables on you. This can manifest in many ways, for example, by asking you about your Story. Be ready for this. Answer the questions with your focus squarely on them. Manage and work on the boundaries at all times. Know where you are in relation to them. Know what the relationship and conversation is at that specific time and place. Don't assume it is simply a continuation of a previous conversation. Be very specific about what your and the other person's expectations are at that moment.

Choose where you are positioning yourself in the relationship. The professional boundary should be that you as the Story-guide do not share your own Stories in depth or detail. To do so would be to burden the Story-sharer with your own struggles. Perhaps the biggest and most damaging unintended consequence of doing so would be that you offer the Story-sharer an easy way to shift the focus away from themselves and the Stories they should be working on, allowing them instead to put you and your Story into the centre. As a Story-guide you will constantly find yourself walking the fine line between showing your own humanity and imperfections, while being conscious of the need to hold an unencumbered, healthy space for the needs of the Story-sharer.

## Projection as a means of driving you away

There are times when the Story-sharer may also project aspects of their old and outdated internal narrative on to the Story-guide. This can be contrived by the Story-sharer as a means of apparently driving you away. Leaving, however, is the last thing you should do. Projection is a form of psychological protection in which the person attributes their own unacceptable thoughts, feelings and behaviours to another person. Below is an example of an intervention to undo the impact of someone's childhood story being projected on to you in your role as

Story-guide, with the clear intention to drive you away. The Story-guide might say to the Story-sharer:

> "I have done a lot of thinking about what is going on between us. You know that I am stubborn and that I am pledged to not let you succeed in driving me away. I know that the next time I see you, the next time you get a message from me, you will try some more. You have your own reasons for doing what you are doing. I think there's a Story there. I really think there's a Story there. I know that you may not be ready to tell me. I know that you may not even be ready to get in touch with it, but I know there is a Story there and one day you will feel safe enough to share it with me, even if you have only the barest outlines of what it is."

This is a strong and full voice of a Story-guide that is saying, "I am not going to let you succeed in driving me away."

As the Story-work progresses and the person starts to let go pieces of the dark side of their childhood story, the scales will start to even out, there will be more balance, the good things that are happening will take on greater weight, and the battle will begin to subside, including any battles with you, the Story-guide.

## The role of consolidation

Time is needed to consolidate changes that have been made by the Story-sharer through the process of Story-work, before entering the final phase of drawing the work to a close. In due course, the Story-sharer will not need the Story-guide in the same way anymore. This is to be welcomed, but carries its own dangers. As you begin to signal during the consolidation phase that the time for drawing the work to a close is approaching, there can be strong and powerful disturbance for the Story-sharer. Do not be surprised if yet another cycle of retrenchment shows itself.

Part of the consolidation involves the Story-sharer being able to get what they need, being clear about what that is, and knowing how much they need the Story-guide to stay engaged in the personal work with them. In a way, the consolidation process is a threat to the inner child, because the adult matures in their relationship with the Story-guide.

This is where the change then must happen, and the inner child has to be able to reflect and say:

> "What does that do for me? Do I still need them? Have I got all the support I need? Can I trust my adult-Self to take care of me?"

All these kinds of questions get stoked up, and need to be put to rest, before the actual end of Story-work.

## The path towards freedom

The missing piece in the puzzle is the search for freedom. This finally comes when we can accept the child, can take them in our arms, can playfully put them on our back, can hold their hand, can have them close by, but at the same time know that we are not that child any longer. In the closing phases of Story-work there are frequently moments when the person may struggle with the last pieces of the jigsaw puzzle in their new internal narrative. They already have an idea of what they are. They can sense their shape and form, because they are able to see the corresponding gaps in the puzzle, but they are not quite able to fill them in yet.

Even though there might not be dramatic answers emerging, the way in which the Story-sharer lets you work with them, the quality and depth of the connection between you, and the way in which you deal with the Story-material itself – all that in itself is a big triumph, and well worth the effort. There is no magic formula, no grandiose revelation, instead it is a carefully sculpted, tenacious process that is moving the person more and more along the path towards freedom.

## Premature endings: The Story-guide

The Story-guide faces a critical question: "Is there a tendency to leave too soon or to stay too long?" Story-guides need to attend closely to this and watch out, for example, for the risk of denying a person their need, because of their own bias towards leaving or drawing things to a close too soon. Therefore, the timing for raising the question about drawing the work to a close is critical. Signposting the ending of the sessions can feel like abandonment, rejection or betrayal to the Story-sharer, especially if you go there too soon. To assist in this transition towards an appropriately timed ending, it is important to help the person to go into Meaning and to encourage them to frame or reframe the Affect, especially if they are experiencing a high level of reactivity to the upcoming end of the Story-work process. Know that sometimes the event of ending the work can be so impactful that it simply is very difficult for the person to do this. This is yet another context where knowledge of the Self is critical for the Story-guide. You need to know yourself, your Practice Model and your personal tendencies in order to hold your ground during the inevitable commotion and confusion around the right way to end the Story-work.

> I remember the first time Michael raised the question about ending my sessions with him. It was premature of him to do so, and his prematurity had a big impact on me. In the midst of the storm of the impact I was experiencing, however, he was so open about his flaws in relation to this. He described his tendency to infuse Affect and feeling with Meaning. So when I was filled with Affect, he was filled with Meaning about my Affect and about his own. As a result, he was thinking less about me, and more about himself thinking about me. He talked about how unfair this was, because it resulted in him making a move to end the sessions much sooner – and way too soon – than if he had been really thinking about me and my needs.
>
> **Sarah, Author**

Not only knowing your own gaps, flaws and preferences, but also being at ease to talk about these in a way that is in service of the Story-sharer is so very important in this work.

> In the aftermath of Michael's premature suggestion that the sessions should end, initially I pulled back and withdrew from him and from the personal work with him. He suggested I give up the sense of bringing the sessions to a close, because if I did end the work, I would be abandoning myself. As a result, after working it through, we set it aside. I was able to see that his proposition had triggered my experience of and reaction to abandonment, and I could see there was a further piece of work for me to do on this. It was a perturbation in our relationship that really shook things up. However, it proved to be such a good perturbation, because things that had been

*underlying abandonment came up to the surface from the
depth of the Story, and it became possible to attend to
the associated triggers and themes.*

**Sarah, Author**

## Actually drawing the work to a close

There is no way to mark the end of such deep work without feeling a loss.

*I knew when it was actually time to end the work with
Michael. The realisation and deep sense of 'knowing'
came to me so clearly and in a really good and
wholesome way. The work to draw things to an end
then began. It took some time to conclude. It was not a
sudden act. We had been through a lot together. It was a
strong relationship.*

**Sarah, Author**

Sometimes you need to hang in there until the person is ready to be done. Be patient. And when the time comes that the person begins to talk about ending, do not be too quick to agree and wrap things up either. Sometimes it takes a little time to help the Story-sharer draw things to a close. Other times the person might shock you a little bit by very suddenly terminating the sessions. Be prepared for your own internal reactions when this happens. The end of the relationship between you is bound to feel like a loss to you too.

As the work comes to a close, the needs of the Story-sharer in relation to the Story-guide change. There is a phase towards the end where the requirement is just to check in, to catch up, and to integrate what they are learning. Consequently, the request for support will be qualitatively different. You will see a change in the way you are working together. You will really be joining one another to find the remaining answers, and this is a step in the right direction. Finally, the Story-sharer starts finding their own answers. The whole question of the balance between dependence and valid need changes.

*As Michael and I closed our work together, we were not
dancing in the streets. I had lost something else and that
did not feel good, but I was OK. It was time to end the
work and it was necessary to feel the loss.*

**Sarah, Author**

## Post-Story-work relationship challenges

*Picture the scene: An illustration*

A person has a childhood story in which they were not seen or heard in their family system. You have done the work through deep knowing and deep relationship to enable them to transform and change the internal narrative that the person has been carrying for a long time. You have represented perfect love in some ways through how you have focused on really being with, seeing, hearing and witnessing them. Fast-forward to the post-Story-work relationship in which they begin to see and experience your own imperfections and flaws. Imagine a moment occurring in which you are triggered into your own high stakes reactivity, and in that instant, in their eyes, you fail to be with, see or hear them. The impact this can have on them is naturally at risk of being disproportionate as a result of the clash with the nature of the previous relationship. Two invisible realities come into contact in moments of this kind, and they can easily throw off sparks.

Rebecca tells the story from her perspective of what happened between she and I when the relationship and boundaries between us began to change:

> Most often people begin work with a Story-guide and
> it is a professional arrangement and contract, which
> ceases at the end of their time working on the childhood
> story. That brings with it its own challenges. But in my
> case, that wasn't what happened. My relationship with
> Sarah changed unexpectedly into a different kind of
> working relationship, in which, instead of me being her
> client [Story-sharer], she became mine in a business I had
> set up. As we neared the end of the contract we found
> ourselves in disagreement about the way something had
> been handled. I had done something in a particular way
> and she held a different view about what should have
> happened and whose responsibility that might have been.
>
> Sarah was someone who had stood by me as I had shared
> my Story. I felt like she knew me more intimately than
> most people ever had, or ever would, and I had always
> felt supported and cared for by her. It was a jolting
> experience as I heard her strongly Oppose me for the first

*time and I suddenly started to question everything I knew
about her. For me, two worlds had collided and I
felt wounded.*

*I threw up a metaphoric steel fence between us. She could
say and do what she wanted. I was immovable under
attack and I would not, under any circumstances, allow
her to connect with my Affect. In the past, this was how
I would eventually end up complying and agreeing with
what others wanted that took me to a place of having self-
sacrificed too much. And this was much more likely with
someone I had grown to care about. I experienced her
efforts to connect with me as manipulative, and I can only
imagine how my tone and behaviour must have changed.*

*I subsequently found out that she was at a point of
working on invoking more Oppose and self-protection in
her own repertoire. The shift from my previous experience,
layered with my own Story, made me perceive it as attack
and manipulation, when I can see quite clearly now, that
it was not. It also revealed one of the dangers of the
relationship between Story-guide and Story-sharer – there
is a perception of depth, but it is one-sided. I knew
relatively little about her Story. I now realise that my frosty
demeanour, immovable stance and aggressive tone may
well have held triggers for her, but I wasn't so aware of
that at the time.*

*We missed each other completely; our two invisible realities
became entangled and our previous relationship as
Story-guide and Story-sharer fuelled a disproportionately
volatile series of interactions.*

**Rebecca, Coach**

As you can hear in Rebecca's account, there can be a feeling of 'mess'
where there is a post-Story-work relationship between Story-sharer and
guide, but it does not have to be this way. It takes careful, painstaking
work on the part of both parties to traverse this territory successfully. Yet
again, careful management of the relational boundary is central to this.
During transition and boundary realignment, the Story-sharer may read
all manner of things into the behaviour of the Story-guide, who then

needs to be closely aware of the potential struggle the person may be experiencing. The job of the Story-guide is to help both to get beyond the struggle, to catch the nonsense of what can arise through shadow-dancing with one another, as the Story-guide withdraws from being a Story-guide and becomes an ordinary person that reveals more about themselves. However, there can be a serious side to the impact for the Story-sharer too. There can be a lingering feeling of loss and separation even though there is a post-Story-work relationship of some kind. At times, both Story-sharer and guide might be drawn back into focusing on the Story-sharer's Story which is not ideal for either of them. In the event of this happening, it is important to Bystand together in Meaning about what has occurred as a reminder of the new relational boundary.

It should also not come as a surprise if the Story-sharer expresses anger, if the Story-guide appears to distance themselves for some time and in some ways is no longer such a strong Protector for the person. The Story-guide gives close-up protection during the Story-work, and so when it is ending, it is no wonder that the Story-sharer may feel deserted by them. The Story-guide needs to consciously create some distance between themselves and the Story-sharer for some time. The idea is to step back in order to avoid inviting an ongoing dependency from the Story-sharer. Whenever there exists a post-Story-work relationship, you both need to manage the situation proactively so that you can come back together in what is now more of a peer-setting, and be even closer. The hope and intention is that the relationship can and will be different from the Story-work setting. By separating in a healthy and wholesome way after the Story-work, it becomes possible for respect and love in the future relationship to become even stronger than before.

## After the work is completed

In all relationships that are very important to the Story-sharer, including the relationship with the Story-guide, there will always be the risk that dark powers can appear suddenly and threaten to undo the hard-won gains from Story-work. In the relationship between Story-sharer and Story-guide, the Story can take over again, and swamp the Story-sharer's reality, swamp the trust, swamp the feeling of connection that seemed to have become so solid between them through the intensive Story-work they have done together. The behavioural response can be extreme and overwhelming in the heat of the moment. The Story-sharer can end up at the Story-guide's throat in a blink. Even if there is a good explanation [and reason] for 'losing it', with strong triggering effects being at work, this requires attention. The question that may need further exploration relates to the fact that the Story-sharer is still vulnerable to those triggers and can be framed in the following way:

> "How responsible are you, in your own growth, for
> commanding the childhood story and its effects, even and
> especially when there are painful triggers?"

One can get caught up again in the old internal narrative emanating out of the childhood story, almost drowning in data about the way in which the old narrative manifests and takes hold. The person can feel that again – despite all the Story-work – they do not have much control over the upwelling childhood emotions in the midst of high stakes. They may need to reach out to you and ask for help to regain control once again. It is as though the person is saying:

> "Pay attention to this, I'm so lost in my Story right now, I need
> your help as my Story-guide to get me back out of it again."

To re-experience the unmodulated impact of the old narrative out of the blue in such a demoralising way so long after completing the Story-work can feel devastating. It can seem as though the experience goes beyond retrenchment somehow, yet, this is what it is. It is yet another manifestation of retrenchment, and it can feel horrendous to be confronted with the strength and power of its impact. Yet the person will come out of it far stronger than they might be able to imagine whilst they are submerged in the experience, so long as the Story-guide remains on an even keel.

The Story-guide needs to have the willingness and presence to 'throw their arms' around the person and call on the Protector. Offer your hand to the person once again. Do not fail them by not doing so. This act will mitigate any negative effects:

> "I am here for you, I will be here for you, put all that is
> happening between us behind us, here is my hand."

You as the Story-guide need to be able to get beyond your own potential muddle and your own reactivity. You cannot change this, you cannot avoid this responsibility even in moments when you are into your own Story and potentially being triggered as a result.

# Chapter 11

## Do Your Own Work Too

### Imperfect love and the
### exceptional Story-guide

*"Knowledge of the Self is the mother of all knowledge. So it is incumbent on me to know myself, to know it completely, to know its minutiae, its characteristics, its subtleties and its very atoms."*

**Kahil Gibran**

### Knowing yourself broadly and deeply

From the very first moment we lock gaze with a Story-sharer, the Story-guide is on a journey of discovery. Every piece of information revealed is telling us something. It comes packaged in all sorts of ways, ranging from the explicit direction of the CEO who 'knows what needs to change', to the covert behavioural tip-offs lurking in the hidden corners of an organisation. It is the tapestry woven from this information that builds a vivid picture directing the Story-guide towards the work to do. But it is all too easy for the Story-guide to get sucked into this vortex of analysis, believing that they are external, independent and, therefore, somehow objectively and impartially examining the presenting symptoms, through the clearest, most high-definition lens there can be. That is, after all, one of the benefits many organisations cite in employing an external consultant to intervene in complex organisational issues.

The truth is that from the moment we first connect with the Story-sharer, we too become part of that system. It is well documented across all areas of scientific endeavour that total objectivity is not possible. The act of observation changes the observed; our presence as Story-guide in itself alters the dynamic of the Story-sharer's engagement with the past. By the same token, what we are seeing, assessing and carefully designing interventions for, is being viewed through our own lens, with all its biases, flaws and imperfections. Much as we might want to believe that our expertise makes us impervious to invisible reality, it is simply not true. The Story-guide who fails to acknowledge that risks, at best, rendering themselves ineffective and, at worst, causing untold damage.

> Take, for example, my own Story that has unfolded in the pages of this book. As you have read, as a survivor of violence in childhood, my behavioural propensities are steeped in a deep desire to build solid relationships with others; to respect, care for and protect them at all costs. It is also one of the reasons why, given the choice, I can be inclined to avoid Opposition. So in entering a system where politeness prevails; where the desire to protect and maintain the status quo, seems impenetrable, I will, without doubt, fail, if unable to create perturbance. Not just create it, but sit with it. I need to purposefully design and facilitate interventions that jolt an individual, team or organisation into a position where the possibility for change finally opens up. Just before that opening happens, in the midst of the perturbance, the environment can be visibly and palpably awash with anxiety and my desire to soothe can pull at me. Without the depth of knowledge I have about my behavioural propensities and what is driving them, then instinctively, I will avoid precisely what might create the very shift in behaviour that is so desperately needed.
>
> **Sarah, Author**

In different ways, we are all subject to a version of these unseen, engrained constraints to our practice. That's why the work to understand your own invisible reality; building that knowledge and insight into a Practice Model, is such vital work, if we are to really be in service of the Story-sharer. But please do not be deceived into thinking that what I am talking about here is just simple self-awareness. The development of a Practice Model is a life's work, reaching deep into the territory of childhood story. We have to go back to those formative moments when behaviours, good and bad, were modelled to us – if not upon us – and when we reacted as frail, vulnerable children, laying down deeply-engrained structures, largely concealed from our own consciousness, and invisible to the outside world. These structures contain the themes that trigger our best and worst behaviours, and they remain relatively unchanged – and for most people completely unspoken about – throughout life. A Story-guide who builds their Practice Model, develops a deep understanding of their own behaviour and expands their tolerance for difference, giving them an enviable communicative repertoire and the ability to safeguard others from the effects of their darker, less desirable behaviours.

> *As a child, I experienced a repeated pattern of behaviour in which violence towards me was preceded by a build-up of questioning, usually rhetorical, which came in rapid fire and left me feeling bewildered, disempowered and flustered. That Story isn't visible to a client, nor should it be. But it is still a structure, which threatens to have a detrimental effect on my behaviour. So as an interventionist, when a barrage of challenging questions rain down on me from a group I'm working with, there's a risk that this will spark, in me, a particularly virulent form of shadow behaviour, with all the potentially damaging and unintended consequences that might bring. Having worked long and hard on my own Practice Model, I know that's not what I'll do. I'm not the liability I could be, if I hadn't done that work on myself.*
>
> **Sarah, Author**

You will be more effective as a Story-guide, once you experience how difficult it is to make a change of this kind. You will be fuller and more nuanced and more powerful as a Story-guide when you struggle with the kinds of things we ask of the Story-sharer. Once you absorb the issues during your own Story-work, you realise there are structures, themes and Stories that parallel their lives and if you can make the changes yourself, you are more than halfway there in the work with them.

## There is no guarantee we do not at times do harm

Of course, it is important to be truly aware and in command of your own behaviour and its background-Story, expertly troubleshooting your occasional foibles as they rise to the surface in certain circumstances. But even more challenging is catching where your well-intentioned and even well-executed behaviours are actually triggering the invisible reality of the Story-sharer, jeopardising any chance of success.

*Perhaps most vivid in my memory is the case of a large organisation who had employed me as a consultant to help them with a raft of issues, which were severely impeding their effectiveness. As soon as I set foot in the building, threats were rife. I was rapidly fed all manner of anecdotes indicating that those who had taken the same path before me had been unsuccessful. People were overtly willing me to fail. This behaviour began to unravel an unspoken and invisible reality starting at the very top of the organisation.*

*Marred by a deeply troubled history and great tragedy, the organisational narrative had been re-written into a more polished and palatable version of the truth. It didn't take long for me to see that the expression of feelings was a rare phenomenon there. It wasn't that they didn't exist – just that a suppression of them was commonplace. They couldn't have known it at the time, but I had the awareness to realise that my natural propensities were likely, left unchecked, to prove my doubters right. My innate desire to create connection and draw out true feelings was likely to be blocked from every angle – no matter how skilful I may have thought I was in that discipline.*

**Sarah, Author**

The design of that particular intervention had to painstakingly take account of an invisible reality that was already partially peeking through layers of visible organisational behaviour. Drawing out what lies in these invisible realities of the client takes creativity, resilience and courage. But more than that, it takes a Story-guide to be knowingly in command of their own Story and the invisible reality that it creates for themselves, because it is that awareness which can transform hazardous and potentially flammable material into an endless source of positive energy to draw upon in service of the client.

*If you are working with leaders and their childhood stories, to truly be in service of another you need to know your own Story, otherwise you could do more harm than good. You need to be at your best and present, not grappling with your own Story.*

**Matthew, Coach**

## Knowing the self: In the moment, in the room

So as a Story-guide, getting in touch with what is happening in the room between yourself and the Story-sharer, and how you are impacted by it is essential. It is like a thermometer. For example, you cannot be of complete service to other people, if you are more concerned with taking care of them than of yourself, nor if you are unable to locate empathy for the people you are working with in any given system. Once that empathy is fully in place you will be able to recognise your feelings, and after a while you learn how to process very, very quickly. A central element of knowing the Self in this context is being aware of what stops you in your tracks and causes reactions in you, as well as knowing how to handle these moments well. To do this, you need to know your own Stories. You need to know what is triggering you and be able to work effectively with the impact of the triggers. That way you are not in danger of getting into a pattern of reactivity that is more a reflection of your own inner child than the adult professional.

> The work on Self is critical for a number of reasons. Obviously, the benefit that it brings for Self, the ability to be more in command, more in touch with your own high stakes behaviours, etc. That work on Self has allowed me to bring a greater level of vulnerability and authenticity to my work as a coach, to my work as a leader and to all my relationships. And they're two things that sometimes get bandied around a lot in leadership circles – but true vulnerability and authenticity are so important to breaking down barriers. And whilst it may feel like you're taking a backward step, actually being able to say, you are not as stoic as you thought, or to admit that you might not be the best you can be at particular times, is so important. It's the ability to connect with your inner child. It's incredibly powerful as a practitioner.
>
> **Mark, Coach**

Childhood story work can be very powerful and moving for the Story-guide as well as the Story-sharer. This makes it necessary for you as the Story-guide to keep a kind of reserve of Affect. You need to feel what is happening in the room, but you also need to be able to ask questions about yourself, about the other and about what is going on in the session. There will be times when you really 'get' and 'feel' a part of the Story, rather than merely understanding it intellectually. It might, for example, be that you really feel – maybe palpably – what a mess life was for the child that today is still inside your client. In these moments, the Story effectively breaks through the reserve of Affect that the Story-guide normally holds, and that allows you to remain appropriately in Meaning in service of the Story-sharer. Such a breaking through of the Story can be very healthy for a Story-guide, because you need to be in touch truthfully with your own feelings. But you cannot allow yourself to 'drown' in the Story. Striking the right balance is a critical skill in being able to connect with compassion, which is a high form of love and essential to Story-work. By the same token, you want the Story-sharer to know enough about you, and who they have chosen to work with, but not so much that you burden them with your own Story.

It is OK to have doubts, or get things wrong on occasion, and to show openly in the sessions that you have imperfections too. You join the person in their process, and struggle with the issues alongside them. You explore what is coming up for them and help them to find ease. You help them to replace the pain they may be experiencing under their old internal narrative with something else, with compassion for the Self, with love, with acceptance.

Not allowing yourself, as Story-guide, to feel what you are really feeling can only short change the Story-sharer. You cannot make a really good learning experience out of it, if you don't allow yourself to be touched. The model we use in Structural Dynamics includes people getting in touch with the impacts they have on others. It is not always inappropriate or dangerous as an interventionist to bring your feelings out, but unless you learn how to express them appropriately – even under high stakes – you cannot be fully effective in helping others. The Story-sharer needs to become aware of how they, with their profiles and Stories, impact other people; and the Story-sharer can only learn about – and eventually gain command over – these phenomena in their own behavioural patterns, if we as Story-guides are able to appropriately model healthy patterns in our interactions with them.

There are different ways that the Story-guide's behavioural preferences and childhood story can make their way into the work with the client. Sometimes it is called upon by the situation, or the Story-guide is called upon directly, to venture into this territory. Learning what to do in the room with a phenomenon while at the same time being strongly impacted by it, is one of the most critical skills for any interventionist.

## The crossing of boundaries

David Kantor, in a meeting of colleagues we were leading, described his concepts of 'epistemic failure' and 'compensatory replacement', which are relevant here for Story-work. Epistemic failure manifests where the boundaries between the personal and professional are violated and harm is done in the process. This happens, mostly without noticing, if we, as the Story-guide, cross into the Story-sharer's world, to make up for the deficits we experienced from our own Stories of loss or missing love. In other words, we subconsciously engage in compensatory replacement, trying to satisfy our own needs, ignoring their needs, and endangering their progress.

My own experience of these phenomena is contained in Chapter 7 and below are examples generously shared by close colleagues and friends that bring these concepts to life:

> The fact that I frequently assert that I will 'do my best' is an indication of my early search for parental, particularly my mum's love, especially when I suspected troubled times. My way to finding that love was to be a 'good girl' and be helping my mother in whatever way I could from a very early age. This dynamic re-established itself when one of my sisters, at the age of 16, became pregnant to the local 'bad boy'. The experience totally changed how our mother related to all of us in the family. It was not in a positive loving way.

> I continued my quest to find my mother's love by being the good girl with even more vigour and with an additional layer of becoming the Protector, not only to my mother and father, but also to the injured, my sister! To this day I find myself helping and protecting, what do I mean by protecting? Well, a sense of protecting others from harm, making things OK for them. I do this with my husband and in the family, constantly trying to broker conversations or taking things on to protect others from hardship.

> How do the two dynamics of helping and protecting show up in my role as an interventionist? Well, actually, the opposite to what I might expect; rather than helping

and protecting clients to stay safe and take cautious or no action with them, I actually and perhaps unconsciously, push them to have conversations with me which they might otherwise retreat from. I think this is a form of 'compensatory replacement' for when I was not able to express my own voice. I kept my own distaste or norms or conventions and rebellion against political and 'statutory' authority. I could not do that in a way which could be seen. I did do it, but undercover, away from the gaze of my parents in case I was found out and would not be viewed as a 'good girl' any longer, and to protect them from any more pain. I wonder if I have ever pushed clients to confront their nemesis when I could have chosen not to do so. And still I find it difficult actually to do so myself! I know for sure that I have done that, I have pushed in this way, but did it do harm? That, I don't know. I am left though wondering, if I automatically go straight for the 'you need to talk this out' route without actually exploring enough what dynamics have led to their current situation.

**Nina, Coach**


My example is about colluding with the system. I have a tendency to gravitate to women in power as opposed to men. In part, this is because male dominant figures trigger high stakes reactions in me that stem from my relationship with my Grandfather in childhood.

I remember one time when I did some intervention work in a team with one female leader, who I believed was very low in Affect, and actually wasn't. In the first intervention, I was so focused on succeeding and pleasing her that I lost the details that the coaching sessions had pulled out. Her high Affect was disabling the team's ability to Oppose. I also didn't want to Oppose her; I wanted to please her and get validation from her. I was seeking a form of compensatory replacement for the absence of this validation while growing up in my own family system.

In the second intervention I knew this, and as a result, on the fly created a sculpting exercise to spatialise the *behavioural structure, and put all of the team in Oppose around a dialogue topical to them, except her.[13] This was facilitated through reframing and re-contracting with her in advance. The outcome? Better awareness of this structurally in the team and permission to Oppose being given for the future. It also felt different and good for me, as she did validate the session and the works' success.*

**Matthew, Coach**

Events of this kind happen all the time; they show up in innumerable ways. They do harm, because they largely sit beneath the surface of our awareness. By bringing them fully into view through deep and rigorous reflective practice – in which we closely examine the choices we make in moments where this crossover occurs – it becomes possible to catch and reframe what could otherwise undo the good we are seeking to do through our work.

## Choosing Affect, Power or Meaning

As a Story-guide, even the language you use to elicit the details from the Story-sharer is already an indication of what you are looking for. It is very important to be aware of this. We do know that peoples' profiles determine much of the language they utilise. This is the case for both Story-sharer and guide. There may, for example, be a tendency on the part of the Story-guide to draw out the childhood story just in the Communication Domain of Affect. That drive to explore in Affect is obviously especially strong, if Affect is the Story-guide's strength or even stuck preference, but it might not be what the client needs most.

It is usually pretty easy for a Story-guide to open up people's sadness, their emotions and their feelings. However, many people get correspondingly easily hooked into and by Affect. Whilst there is a need to express it,

---

13 Sculpting to spatialise a structure in Structural Dynamics intervention involves using the physical environment including objects and the positioning of people in relation to one another to bring a structure or dynamic to life in the room. For example, you might ask one person to strike a pose in the way they are standing in which they are setting a direction [making a Move] and another to respond using their body in such a way as to correct that direction [providing an Oppose]. You might then ask the pair to keep repeating this until the pattern is visible and felt by them and by others in the room.

the constant voicing of the feelings can keep the Story-sharer stuck and trapped in their Story for years. To counter this, it is critical to be able to elicit responses or in-depth explorations of what is happening in the person's life using all three Communication Domains:

- How do you feel about that? [Affect]

- What do you think about that? [Meaning]

- What do you want to do about that? [Power]

Listen to the person whose Story you are eliciting. If they speak Power, you have to decide whether you meet them in Power, or in Meaning or Affect. But you also need to be aware of your own preferences and biases.

## Switching and moving

The Story-guide needs to develop a strong skill-set for equipping Story-sharers to switch in and out of their Story; light to shadow, shadow to light; deep in Story to light in Story. Being able to facilitate a shift between Affect and Meaning is a critical mechanism for enabling this kind of switching. The expression of feelings is important, but so is the ability to make meaning, to understand the Story, how it manifests through the internal narrative etc.

> Michael constantly switched between Affect and Meaning in the sessions and had me do the same too. Even in the midst of the conversation I could often really hear him guiding me in this way throughout. It is remarkable how he enabled me to make this move, but it is also remarkable how able I was to go from real and acute distress and high Affect right into thinking together in Meaning and talking in Power within a very short space of time. He would do this especially whenever it was a very difficult session.
>
> **Sarah, Author**

This experience of switching with ease between Communication Domains is important, because we know how powerful Affect can be when we are in the midst of it. Giving this experience of switching out of Affect with ease to the person you are working with on their Story, you create the opportunity for them to connect with the reality that Affect will always pass. It is impermanent, even though it does not always feel that way when you are caught up in it. This ability to consciously and knowingly switch and move is integral to your work as Story-guide, and you need to be able to do this for yourself too. Therefore, you must also know what your best voice is when dealing with people's very darkest material in their Story. Will it be Affect, Power or Meaning? But to be effective, you need to have range in your profile. You need to think about the language you should best use in critical moments, when you are trying to bring change about in people's lives, and not be carried forward by your own preferences only. You need to know how that very individual Story-sharer will hear your own best voice through their biases, and what kind of impact it might have on them. Consider, for example, the impact of Open Affect on Closed Power or Random Meaning on Closed Affect.

In addition, you must know that your own nightmares from your Story impact on your choice of voice in the room with others, not always positively. So for example:

> I know that my own choice of Affect may actually be detrimental to a group of people whose best voice is Power. I am at ease in being in a room with people breaking down in Affect and in Meaning, but less so when it is a group that is breaking down in Power. I have speculated about where that comes from. I believe it emanates from the powerless child who was trapped under the table terrified of her parents and their use of Power back then.
>
> **Sarah, Author**

## Comfort with tears

When beginning to share their Story more deeply the Story-sharer does, of course, get thrown back in time, and this can create perturbance for them as well as for you. There can be a powerful release of emotion as a result of the time you spend together in the Story. It is almost as if stored up fears, tears and emotion get unplugged. There can be a lot of nervousness on the part of the Story-guide about the expression of emotion through tears by the Story-sharer. In part, this is profile driven. We have to look at ourselves more closely in relation to how Affect shows up in our own behavioural preferences, and what our own Stories are in relation to these patterns, so that we can truly be in service of the people we are working with.

To help with this, we can also make up a different kind of account about the expression of tears. They are often good tears, a release and a relief. The account could be that the tears have been stored up, and now finally here is somebody the person can truly call upon, who is listening to them, who knows them deeply, and who really cares about them. This is what is enabling the tears to flow at last. It could also sometimes be that tears are an expression of feeling the relief that is coming from liberating a new internal narrative.

## Sharing your own childhood story

A lot of people who act as coaches and interventionists tend to focus their attention on others and do not share their own childhood story. As a result, they themselves do not have the community of trust that comes with sharing their own Story with their colleagues, and yet they spend a lot of effort on creating that trust for other people. In sharing your childhood story with other colleagues, you create a family of protectors, which is a lovely thing. Being able to do that reciprocally between colleagues is helpful and mutually supportive too. When sharing your childhood story with your colleagues, they are getting an awareness of your shadow behaviour and when it comes in – for example, in high stakes – are then better able to support you, as you work to change your involuntary dark patterns. Knowing the childhood story that sits behind somebody's [damaging] reactivity is really helpful when trying to be supportive in change.

It can also potentially be a good thing – even a very good thing – to share your childhood story with the leaders you are accompanying as Story-guide. But it can never be in such a way as to burden them with it. It can only be in service of them, as they work on their own Story. The call is yours. This is a relational model, therefore, as a Story-guide, you are right in it, right in the centre of the relational field. It is very real, very challenging, and very rewarding when you see the fruits.

# A postscript

*A Story of Imperfect Love and Extraordinary Transformation.*

I was busy formulating the final steps in my plan of work on my Story and its accompanying narrative with Michael, when my father had a fall that he did not recover from. In his last days, he redeemed himself for me. He was not frightened anymore. In his death and dying, he was courageous. He had agency in his dying and this surprised and comforted me. Something new happened, he showed me something new. I was so proud of the way he died.

I sat by his side in the hospital. I spoke to him and found myself saying:

> *"No matter what happened, I am healthy and whole and I am here with you, supporting you as you are dying."*

I felt at peace. I had done my best. I had taken care of him. I had taken care of myself too. I had survived the Story. I had done something so very good with it.

This was my eulogy for him:

May my voice sing out into this space as I honour the peace, liberation and release I finally began to find in my relationship with Dad over the past few months. Importantly, today marks a firm beginning in the writing of a new narrative of my childhood.

Mine has been a journey that has taken place over more than five decades and one that has finally, finally culminated in my being able to both acknowledge and celebrate my successful transformation of past hurt and suffering.

With unstinting love and support from you, Patrick, and enduring patience and love from David, Ad and Sonia, from Karl, Bob and so many friends, I have been able to really lean into the process of letting go and, in so doing, have been able to really honour the past and not allow it to impact so negatively on me.

In some ways Dad's death was a shock, and yet I believe that as I began to let go, so did he. Today, there is deep sadness as just two of us stand here alone bearing witness to his passing, yet there is also a profound feeling of release and relief.

Dad didn't really know how to love or be loved, but no matter which way I look back and no matter how much pain and suffering I endured at his hands, I bow to him as I say goodbye.

I bow to him with an open heart that is filled to overflowing with compassion.

I bow to him for the 70-hour weeks he worked to try to put enough food on our table when we were small.

I bow to him and thank him for his unstinting dedication to Mum and his care of her right to the bitter end.

I bow to him with a smile in my heart for the moments of love I saw him express for our children when they were babies, the traffic light jellies he made them which they so adored and the £5 notes he would press into my hand to give them for birthdays and Christmas long after they were grown up to be the beautiful young men they are now.

I bow to him with the deepest gratitude for the moments in the closing hours of his life in which he reached out to me and thanked me for caring for him and in which he was able to find the courage to let go.

With grace, compassion and respect I say goodbye to him, thankful for what I learned through it all and appreciative for how I have put that learning to use in the world.

Goodbye Dad, farewell.

May you rest in peace now.

May you be well and happy and free from fear.

May you walk free.

**David Alan Braybon**
26th May 1930 –20th April 2014

# Recommended reading

Ackerman, D. [2012] The Brain on Love, *New York Times*, March 25th

Angelou. M. [2005] *The Collected Autobiographies of Maya Angelou*, Virago

Bachelard, G. in Tobin, D. [1999] *Passage to the Center: Imagination and the Sacred in the Poetry of Seamus Heaney*, The University Press of Kentucky

Baldwin, C. [2005] *Storycatcher*, New World Library

Bausch, W. J. [2015] *Storytelling, Imagination and Faith*, Clear Faith Publishing

Bennett, A. [2014] *Arnold Bennett - The Great Adventure: "Any change, even a change for the better is always accompanied by drawbacks and discomforts."* Stage Door Publishing

Bornstein, D. [2016] Putting the Power of Self-Knowledge to Work, *New York Times*

Brooks, D. [2015] The Year of Unearthed Memories, *Harvard Business Review*, 15th December

Brown, B. [2015] *Rising Strong*, Penguin Random House

Campbell, J. [1990] *The Hero's Journey*, Harper Collins

Cohen, R. [2015] The Presence of the Past, *New York Times*

Davies, A. [2015] *Be Your Own Fairy Tale*, Watkins

Drake, D. B. [2015] *Narrative Coaching: Bringing our New Stories to Life*, CNC Press

Freud, S. & Hall, G. [2016] *A General Introduction to Psychoanalysis*, CreateSpace Independent Publishing Platform

George, B. et al. [2007] Discovering your Authentic Leadership, *Harvard Business Review*

Gibran, K. [2013] *The Prophet,* Vintage Classics

Gilbert, P. & Andrews, B. [1998] *Shame: Interpersonal Behaviour, Psychopathology and Culture,* Oxford University Press

Hill, S. et al. [2004] 'We've all come together as one - prisoners, staff and managers': Prison Dialogue as a means of facilitating patient/public involvement and implementing new standards in prison healthcare, *Prison Service Journal,* No. 151, 30-35

Hill, S. [2014] 'Knowing Yourself Broadly and Deeply: A Commentary', *The Training Journal,* pp19-20

Hughes, S. [2013] What does my childhood have to do with my leadership? *Huffington Post*

Isaacs, W. [1999] *Dialogue and the Art of Thinking Together,* Doubleday

Johnson, R. [1994] *Owning Your Own Shadow: Understanding the Dark Side of the Psyche,* Bravo Ltd

Jones, R. [2016] The Family Dynamics We Grew Up with Shape How We Work, *Harvard Business Review*

Kabat-Zinn, J. [2016] *Mindfulness for Beginners: Reclaiming the Present Moment and Your Life,* Sounds True

Kahane, A. [2010] *Power and Love: A Theory and Practice of Social Change,* Berrett-Koehler

Kantor, D. [1985] *Couples Therapy, Crisis Induction and Change, Casebook of Marital Therapy,* pp21-71, The Guildford Press

Kantor, D. [1999] *My Lover, Myself: Self Discovery Through Relationship,* Riverhead Books

Kantor, D. & Lehr, W. [2003] *Inside the Family,* Meredith Winter Press

Kantor, D. [2012] *Reading the Room,* Jossey Bass

Kantor, D. [2014] *'Working with Invisible Reality',* The Training Journal

Kurtz, C. [2014] *Working with Stories in Your Community or Organisation*, Kurtz-Fernhout Publishing

Kornfield, J. [2002] *A Path with Heart*, Rider

Liedloff, J. [1989] *The Continuum Concept*, Penguin

Lustbader, W. [2011] *Life Gets Better: The Unexpected Pleasures of Growing Older*, Tarcher/Penguin

Metzger, D. [1992] *Writing for your life: A Guide and Companion to the Inner Worlds*, Harper-Collins e-books

Miller, A. [2001] *The Truth Will Set You Free*, Perseus Books Group

Miller, A. [2005] *The Body Never Lies: The Lingering Effects of Cruel Parenting*, WW Norton Ltd.

Mindell, A. [2014] *Sitting in the Fire*, Deep Democracy Exchange

Moonchild, M [2016] *Jung: An Introduction into the World of Carl Jung: The Shadow, The Archetypes and Symbols*, Createspace Independent Publishing Platform

Ober, S. [2015] *Unleashing the Power of Your Story*, Smashwords

Oelrich, I. L. [2015] *The New Story: Storytelling as a Pathway to Peace*, Matador Books

Piaget, J. [1972] *Psychology of the Child*, Basic Books

Pinkola Estés, C. [2008] *Women Who Run With The Wolves*, Rider

Poe, E. A. [2014] *The Complete Tales and Poems of Edgar Allan Poe*, Race Point Publishing

Schwartz, C. [2016] *In the Mindfields: Exploring the New Science of Neuropsychoanalysis*, Vintage

Simmons, P. [2003] *Learning to Fall: The Blessings of an Imperfect Life*, Bantam

Solms, M. [2015] *The Feeling Brain: Selected Papers on Neuropsychoanalysis*, Karnac Books

Stern, J. [2010] *Denial: A Memoir of Terror*, Harper Collins

Wheatley, M. [2005] *Finding our Way: Leadership for an Uncertain Time*, Berrett-Khoehler

Winnicott, D. W. [1986] *Home is Where We Start From*, Penguin

Winnicott, D.W. [2000] *The Child, The Family and The Outside World*, Penguin

Winnicott, D. W. [2006] *The Family and Individual Development*, Routledge

Winterson. J. [2011] *Why Be Happy When You Could Be Normal*, Random House

Yalom, I. D. [1985] *The Theory and Practice of Group Psychotherapy*, Basic Books

Yalom, I. D. [2003] *The Gift of Therapy: An Open Letter to a New Generation of Therapists and their Patients*, Piatkus

Zweig, C & Abrams, J. [1990] *Meeting the Shadow: The Hidden Power of the Dark Side of Human Nature*, Jeremy P Tarcher

# Acknowledgements

There are so many people to honour and thank who joined me in the writing of this book. When I started out, I could never have envisaged just what it would take to bring the ideas and experiences to life in words, nor could I have imagined the extraordinary generosity, care and commitment from so many colleagues, friends and family.

I shall always be indebted to David Kantor who was my mentor, business colleague and, as he once described himself to me, 'virtual Father'. He was like the long lost loving parent who waits at the end of every unhappy child's street. His determined and indefatigable love and support saw me through so much as I wrestled with my own Story-work and I will always feel blessed to have found him. We battled a lot, we laughed a lot and we talked a lot. We also did such important work that was integral to the creation of the book. In my opinion, his theory of Structural Dynamics has not yet attained the recognition it deserves and I hope that in some small way, this book will play a part in rectifying that.

Without hesitation or complaint, Tony Melville read drafts of the book more times than anyone else and untiringly gave me feedback every time. From the earliest manuscripts and my stuttering attempts at expressing myself in writing he gave endless encouragement to stick with it and urged me to remember the importance of my voice and my Story being heard. His confidence in me throughout it all has been like an anchor during times of self-doubt. Rachel Horton-Smyth willed me over the line to publication and gave me so much love and big-hearted support. She constantly urged me to have conviction that I really could write this and guided me through the sharing of her own wonderful talent as a writer. I am profoundly thankful for the tireless and rigorous way she worked on everything from the design of the cover to the crafting and formatting of the final version of the book, without which it would still be on my laptop. Donata Caira shared her great wisdom and skill as a practitioner with me in the later stages of the book. Her expression of emotion on reading it for the first time will stay with me forever. She helped me to see and viscerally appreciate that I really was on to something important.

Klaus Hermann has been an extraordinary Editor and generous friend to me. His brilliant mind and attention to detail has served the book so incredibly well. He stretched my brain to its fullest extent urging me on to think creatively and rigorously about the concepts and their application. Not once did he complain at my frequently idiosyncratic use of grammar and punctuation. He gently and assiduously offered correction and guidance time and time again.

Bob Henry, Paul Lawrence and Mark Boyd gave invaluable editing feedback on later drafts of the book and really made me think in new and different ways to improve the accessibility of the content and the reader's experience. Alex Thomas worked with us to layout the book and cover, I am grateful to him for the great way he engaged with us from the outset, as well as for the work he did.

At their wonderful 'Business Book-writing Bootcamp' in Rhode Island, Sheila Heen and Douglas Stone created the most amazing learning environment and provided such inspiration, craft and creativity. The experience and memory of learning with them alongside Kathryn Stanley, Peter Hiddema, Marsha Acker, Diana Patton and Phil Buchanan is very special. Thank you also for the moments of beautiful tenderness as I began to share my writing. Hearing my voice sing out into the room and then looking up to see and receive your reactions impacted on me very deeply. The impromptu 'BBB blues song' by Diana and Doug was also quite something!

To my colleagues and friends who have walked alongside me throughout the whole process of writing the book and have contributed to it in innumerable untold ways – Scott Downing, Sarah Barnes, Jessica Hobbs, Kieran White, David Leese, Gillien Todd, Adam Menz, Kathryn Stanley, Marsha Acker, Marcelo Agolti, Mel Glover and Claire Radley – I am so grateful for every word of encouragement you have given me, for every contribution you have made, for every thought you have stimulated in me, for every conversation we have had about our Stories along the way.

Personally, surviving my Story has not been easy at times but I have done so because of the enduring deep love, presence and generosity of Ad Brugman, Sonia Moriceau, Karl Gregory and Bob Henry. Their support and teaching will stay with me always. I am also grateful to Danny Blyth who has provided me with such gentle and wise care as I have traversed the twists and turns of writing the book and at times struggled with the toll it has taken on me physically and emotionally. He's been hugely supportive.

My final and most important thanks are to my family: my children Thomas, Joshua and Benjamin who motivate me every day to be the person I am, my closest friend and 'virtual sister', Michele Biyilingiro, who stood by me and loved me from the moment we first met at the tender age of sixteen. And finally, my husband Patrick, for whom there are simply not enough words to describe. He is singularly the most generous, loving and kind man I have ever known. He has comforted me in the darkest of times, has danced with me in the lightest of times and has never once waivered in his love for me. One thing that's for certain is that I've not always made it easy for him to do that either! It is his absolute belief in me that gave me the confidence and strength to roll up my sleeves, do the work on myself and share it with others through this book.

# Holding Out A Hand To You, The Reader

As you reach the end of the book, I want to hold out a hand to you, the reader, and invite you to continue what you have started. I wonder what has come up for you, as you have thought about this whole territory of childhood story? It can be such a tender and tough journey of discovery, but one that is frequently filled with so many insights, ideas and potential.

The book began with me posing a challenge to you, to roll up your sleeves and go to work on your own Story. This is one path that you might decide to take. Another might involve you working with others. This could be leaders you are coaching, colleagues you are working alongside, or friends and family members you are close to. Whatever route you take, I wish you a productive, and generative experience. I also hold out a hand of support in the form of ongoing connection, opportunity and guidance. If this is something that you would like to explore further, please go to: www.dialogix.co.uk/childhoodstory/ for more information. I very much hope to see you there.


**Sarah Hill**

Printed in Great Britain
by Amazon

67885148R00129